Ryu's Misadventures Abroad

Revised Edition

Koji Uenishi

FUKURO SHUPPAN Publishing
ふくろう出版

はしがき

本テキストは，学習者が英語に対して更に興味を抱いて学習に励み，一層英語力向上に繋ぐことができるように考えて作成したものです。本書の特徴としては，以下の点が挙げられます。

・筆者の実体験を基にした海外旅行体験記

まず，本書のすべての内容は，筆者が実体験をした内容を基にして，作成されています。龍（Ryu）という登場人物が，海外旅行をしていく内容で楽しく読む事ができるように工夫されています。6 ユニット，18 章の構成となっており，アジア 3 か国（中国・スリランカ・ベトナム）とイギリス，カナダ，アメリカ（フロリダ・ハワイ）を龍が旅する内容です。しかも，本書の最大の特徴は，単なる海外旅行というものではなく，タイトル「Ryu's Misadventures Abroad」でお分かりのように，主人公龍が，楽しい経験ばかりでなく，様々なほろ苦い海外体験もしていきます。具体的には，スリランカで食べたものが当たり，病院に入る体験をすることなどがあります。このように，実際に筆者が体験したことを疑似体験しながら，英語学習を進める事ができるので，学習者も一層興味を持って英文を読んでいくことができます。

・異文化理解的な要素

本書の内容は，海外での異文化体験的な要素も取り入れられています。例えば，先ほど述べた簡易タクシーでの運転手とのやり取りは，スリランカでの旅行体験で見られ，スコットランドでは，チケットがとりにくい「Tattoo Festival」という行事に参加した内容が提示されています。また，ベトナムでは船上観光をしながら異文化体験をします。ハワイでは，ワイキキビーチやダイヤモンドヘッド登山のことが記載されています。このような異文化理解の要素も取り入れた内容となっていて，学習者に英文内容への関心を高めるようになっています。更に，筆者が現地で撮影した写真付きで，学習できるようにしていますので，異文化的要素を視覚的にも学びやすくなっています。

・<u>総合的な英語力を伸長する内容構成</u>

最後に，学習者の総合的な英語力を伸ばすための英文内容構成です。具体的には，各章とも英文見開き 2 ページの長さとなっています。約 800 語から 1000 語の語彙数を使用し，少し長めの英文としています。これは，長文は少し苦手という学習者でも，楽しく英文を読み，今後英字新聞や小説が読み易くなる一つのきっかけとなるように作成しています。また，英文の後の各問題も 4 技能を網羅した内容構成になっています。具体的には，語彙に始まり，リスニング，リーディング問題，スピーキングを視野に入れた問題，文法，最後にライティング問題にも取り組めるようにしています。特に，スピーキングの問題では，本文の内容をベースにしたダイアログ形式の穴埋め問題を解いたあと，ペアワークができるように工夫しています。学習者が英文内容を把握した後で，龍になりきって海外疑似体験をしてもらいたいと思います。

以上が本書の内容説明であります。

今回，このテキストを刊行するに当たり，Charles McHugh 先生には英文校正をして頂き，本当に感謝に堪えません。また，ふくろう出版の亀山さんには一方ならぬご尽力を頂いたことに，この場を借りてお礼申し上げます。

2022 年 3 月　　　　筆　者

Ryu's Misadventures Abroad

Contents

Unit 1 China

Unit 1 China Chapter 1 Beijing Opera

It was past six o'clock when it was time for Ryu's presentation. Ryu felt relieved to see only a few participants who came to listen to his paper. He had a negative feeling that the more audience members, the more difficult questions he would be asked. Anyway, he thought he would have to manage to finish his presentation. His professor and friend were there in the audience to support him. This was his first presentation at an international conference using the Power Point program. Therefore, he had butterflies in his stomach before he started. Once the presentation started, he became calmer and calmer. Once in a while he was just reading his paper, but he finished the 20-minute presentation satisfactorily. It was time for questions, and unexpectedly there were only simple questions that Ryu was able to answer.

After the conference, everyone took a taxi swiftly and rushed to see a classical Chinese opera, called kyougeki in Japanese, at a famous theater in Beijing. It was supposed to start at 6 p.m., so there was not ample time before it started. Of course, being in the taxi, they could not possibly rush to

Beijing Opera

the theater. The taxi driver drove wildly as if their anxiousness was conveyed to him. He overtook other cars, often by driving in a lane which, seemingly, was not part of the road. They arrived at the theater and decided to take special seats which his professor had recommended. These seats were 180 yuan per person and they were much more expensive than the other seats in the theater because they allowed them to sit closer to the stage. The female staff members soon brought an oshibori, a rolled, refreshing hand towel, to them. Then they served them Chinese tea with some sweets, which tasted rather good.

After the musical started on the stage, Ryu was quickly enchanted by the beautiful heroine, who gave a splendid performance in a high-pitched voice. Since the actors were speaking in Chinese, Japanese spectators had to read the translation on the large screen on the right side of the stage to understand the development of the story. When Ryu paid too much attention to the English subtitle on the screen, he tended to look away from this great attraction. Therefore, he had to rapidly move his eyes from the far-right of the screen to the stage to see their brilliant performance. It is easier to read the subtitles on a TV or at a movie theater because people don't have to shift their eyes. They just look in the same direction on the screen ahead of them. Eventually Ryu got so tired of just moving his eyes both to see their performance and to read the subtitles that he jerked his neck back and forth so as to keep up with the story in English. He wished it would be possible to use each eye independently.

Regarding the subtitles, Ryu came across strange translations and spelling errors once in a while. As he remembered, the one letter space before apostrophe (') was a little strange. As he noticed later, this was written on the signs in front of restaurants, too. An example is 'I can 't follow you ...' He didn't know exactly whether or not that would be acceptable.

In the middle of the story, there was a scene in which a beautiful woman and a sailor talked to each other on a boat. Ryu felt very impressed to see it because their performance was comical and attractive. It looked as if they were riding on a boat in the sea, by moving their bodies up and down and swinging them back and forth. He wanted to show his children this kind of splendid performance at the theater in China some day.

After that, they had dinner at a restaurant on the first floor of the same building. There were a lot of compartments where groups of customers could privately enjoy talking and dining in a relaxed way, like at a Japanese bar called 'izakaya'. They drank a toast to their great success in their presentations at the conference. Everybody was very happy to finish it and drank beer. They ate a lot of Chinese food, as well. They were laughing and loudly talking over the news at the conference and their personal stories with jokes because of their relief after the presentations and the easy flow of alcohol. But who expected what would happen to him that night?

Then they were trying to go back to the hotel and asked some of the taxi drivers to drive there, showing thier hotel brochure. Unexpectedly, all the drivers refused to drive to the hotel. "Refused? That's unbelievable!" Ryu thought. He imagined the drivers did not clearly understand the way to the hotel or they might have been too lazy to drive at night. Ryu reentered the theater and asked guards to negotiate for them to take a taxi, using nonverbal language. One of them went through the entrance and approached one of the taxi drivers. Ryu and his professor followed the guard

Beijing Opera(2)

and were watching the negotiation from a little distance away. The guard opened a door of the taxi for them, which implied they would be able to get in. Ryu thought in his mind, "What a relief! It's a deal!" Finally, they traveled back to their hotel safe and sound by taxi.

Vocabulary Check

英単語に合う意味を右の日本語から選び，(　　　)に記号を記入しなさい。

1 overtake	(　　　　　)	a. 追い越す
2 refreshing	(　　　　　)	b. ぐいとねじる
3 enchant	(　　　　　)	c. 魅了する
4 high-pitched	(　　　　　)	d. 喜劇の
5 subtitle	(　　　　　)	e. 非言語の
6 splendid	(　　　　　)	f. 結局
7 eventually	(　　　　　)	g. かん高い
8 jerk	(　　　　　)	h. 素晴らしい
9 comical	(　　　　　)	i. 字幕
10 nonverbal	(　　　　　)	j. さわやかな，すっきりさせる

Listening Section　英文をよく聞いて，英語で答えよう。

1 ______________________________

2 ______________________________

3 ______________________________

4 ______________________________

Reading Comprehension

本文をよく読んで，次の問いに日本語で答えよう。

1 プレゼン前とプレゼンが始まった後の龍は，どんな様子でしたか。

2 京劇を見る前に，女性スタッフは何をしてくれましたか。

3 言語的な観点から，龍が気づいたことは何ですか。

4 美しい女性と船乗りが話す場面を見て，龍が感動したのは何故ですか。

Speaking Section

本文に合うように空所を埋めよう。但し，下線部には 2 語以上入る。その後，龍（Ryu）になったつもりで，パートナー（A）と対話をしてみよう。

<Part 1>

A: What did you see in Beijing, Ryu?

Ryu: I saw a ______________________________.

A: How did you like it?

Ryu: It was fantastic. I loved it. But we spent a lot of money to see it.

A: Why was that?

Ryu: We selected ______________________________ to see it.

A: Were there some staff members to guide you to the seat?

Ryu: Yes. The female staff members brought (   ) and served us ______________________________ with some (   ).

A: Oh, I see. How did you like the food?

Ryu: It tasted ______________________________.

A: By the way, how was the Chinese opera?

Ryu: I was enchanted by the ______________________________.

A: Whoa! I now feel like watching the opera, as well.

<Part 2>

A: Ryu, did you have a good time at the theater?

Ryu: Yes, but I became tired there.

A: Why were you tired?

Ryu: I had to pay attention to the ______________________________ on the screen.

A: I think you can read them easily.

Ryu: No, no. It was hard for me to do that, because I had to ______________ ______________ from the far-right of the screen to the stage quickly to see the ______________________________.

A: I see now.

Ryu: I wish I could have used my ______________________ independently.

A: You can say that again. How about their performance?

Ryu: I was so impressed by a certain scene when their performance was both (   ) and (   ).

A: Tell me the impressive scene, Ryu.

Ryu: Well, it was the scene where a (   ) was talking to a beautiful woman ____________________________ in the sea.

A: Wow! Next time let's go to Beijing together.

Grammar Section

ここでは関係詞の学習をしよう。関係詞には関係代名詞と関係副詞がある。

まず，関係代名詞には **which, that, who, whom, whose** などがある。基本的に前の先行詞を説明するために修飾して使用される。原則的に人の場合，**who (whom, whose)**を使用し，物の場合 **which (whose)** を使用する。**that** はどちらの場合にも使用される。本文中の例文を見てみよう。

He was driving in a lane **which** was not part of the road.

この英文では，関係代名詞（which）の前の先行詞が物（lane）であるから which が使用されている。

また，関係副詞には where, when, why, how などがあり，先行詞によって使われる関係副詞が異なる。先行詞が「場所」の場合は where,「時」の場合は when,「理由」（reason）の場合は why となる。なお，how の場合は先行詞なしで使用する。本文中の例文を見てみよう。

There were a lot of compartments **where** groups of customers could privately enjoy talking and dining in a relaxed way. （グループのお客がリラックスしてプライベートで会話や食事を楽しめる多くの仕切りがあった。）

この英文では，関係副詞の前の先行詞が compartments で場所を示すものであるため，where が使われている。

上記の英文では，全て制限（限定）用法となっているが，次の英文の例のように非制限（継続）用法での使用もある。特徴は関係詞の前に（,）がある。非制限用法の場合は，前の先行詞の補足的な説明となっている。例文を見てみよう。

Ryu was quickly enchanted by the beautiful heroine, **who** gave a splendid performance.

（龍はすぐにその美しいヒロインに見とれていた。なぜなら彼女は素晴らしい演技をしたから）

Arrange Words

（　　　）内の語を並べ替えて，正しい英文にしよう。

1 This is one of the most (seen, have, scenes, ever, I, magnificent, that).

2 The big thatched house, (brought, famous, was, where, writer, up, the), is now a memorial building.

3 There are some students in his class (to, teacher, become, English, want, an, who).

Writing Section

ここでは次の英語表現を学ぼう。

「許可」を示す表現を学習しよう。「**allow** 人 **to** ～」と「**permit** 人 **to** ～」である。どちらも「人が～するのを許す」という意味であるが，後者の「permit」を使用したほうが「公式に許可する」意味合いが強い。本文中の例文を見てみよう！

These seats allowed them to sit closer to the stage.

受身の形では，**be allowed to** ～と **be permitted to** ～である。

We were allowed to smoke in the designated places.

（私たちは指定された場所では，煙草を吸うのを許された。）

People are not permitted to park their cars along the busy street.

（彼らは賑やかな通りでは，車を駐車することを許可されていない。）

それでは，学習した英語表現を使って練習しよう。次の状況で英文を書いてみよう。

1　あなたは，友人の啓太（Keita）と映画を見に行っています。その友人が食べ物を持ち込もうとしていると，あなたは飲食物持ち込み禁止の張り紙があるのに気づきました。友人にこのことを Keita, look at the notice. We...で始めて，英語で表現してみよう。

2　あなたは，友人と車でコンサートを見に行きました。友人が駐車スペースを探しています。あなたは，たまたま一つ開いている場所を見つけました。このことを permit を使い，Look at the space. We ...で始めて，英語で表現してみよう。

Dictation Section

英語を聞いて書き取ってみよう。その英文の意味も書こう。

1 ______________________________

和訳（　　　　　　　　　　　　　　　　）

2 ______________________________

和訳（　　　　　　　　　　　　　　　　）

3 ______________________________

和訳（　　　　　　　　　　　　　　　　）

Unit 1 China Chapter 2 Sightseeing and Hotel (1)

First, Ryu decided to go to the Palace Museum in Beijing. They took a subway to the closest station to the museum and walked toward it along the street. The fare was so reasonable that they could go wherever they wanted to, only paying three yuan. It was then equivalent to about 50 yen in Japanese currency.

Walking on the street, they were really concerned about 'smog' which covered the whole city of Beijing. Ryu thought the air pollution surely would damage their health. While he was talking to his professor, they walked into the park which had a serene atmosphere and helped them calm down.

Ryu saw citizens talking merrily here and there in the park. As they were walking through the park, suddenly the historical museum appeared before them. It was located near the entrance to the Palace Museum. Ryu happened to find a small souvenir shop in front of the gate. Since the city was covered with smog, they were really worried about maintaining their good health. They entered the shop in order to purchase masks to protect themselves from inhaling polluted air, which could lead to bad health. Ryu,

The Palace Museum in Smog

using gestures, asked a female shop employee if they sold masks there. She showed them the ones that civilians wore to block 'bird flu' in South East Asia and China. Ryu and his professor thought it would be better than nothing and they bought some masks. Wearing the masks, they walked around the vast palace precincts to see the beautiful palace and old-time artistic works in the buildings.

The taxi got them back to the hotel at 10:30 p.m. or so. They decided to get together in the lobby at six the next morning in a bid to do some early sightseeing. Ryu went into his room and turned on the TV to watch CNN News. He was just looking at the TV without trying to know the content of the news. As reported the day before, suicide bomb terrorism and bird flu problems in developing countries were on the TV. Ryu slowly changed into casual clothes and looked over the presenters' manuscripts he obtained at the conference that day.

After a while, Ryu thought it was about time to take a bath and go to bed to remove fatigue. The bathtub was not nearly as deep as a traditional Japanese bath. He thought he couldn't make himself comfortable in such a shallow bath since he could not soak like in a Japanese bath. He peeped into the bathtub and first washed it out using the shower. Then, he began to run hot water. That was the beginning of his nightmare. Hot water from the faucet was sent roaring into the bathtub. Imagining he could relax in the tub in 30 minutes, when the bath would become full, Ryu lay back on his bed and began to watch TV again. The male anchor on the CNN News critically reported different news such as the former President Obama's speech on economic policy. He was so fed up with such news reports that he lay down on the bed to get rid of fatigue from attending the conference. He intended to be on the bed for only a short time. Ryu probably felt a huge sense of relief after his presentation. Before he knew it, he began to take a nap on the bed and shortly fell soundly asleep there. Meanwhile, the hot bath water was shooting out fast from the faucet, regardless of his deep sleep. That was his worst luck.

It was about one and a half hours later that Ryu woke up on the bed for no reason. He might have been concerned about the hot water flowing into the bath on a subconscious level. At that moment he heard something running fast from somewhere. He tried to attentively listen to the loud sound in order to make sure what it was. It took a moment to focus on the noise because he was still half asleep. His senses came back to normal, little by little. "Oh, this is WATER! I left the water running," Ryu heard in his mind. He jumped off of the bed quickly and tried to head for the bathtub. Then, he felt unpleasant and damp under his feet as if he were stepping on a water-saturated sponge. He looked down at the floor around his feet. The color had turned from light to dark blue around his bed, because the carpet was soggy from the bath water.

Ryu headed for the bathroom, splashing on the soggy floor. Like a waterfall, the water was rapidly flowing down from the raised bathroom into the bedroom. When he opened the door to the bathroom, it was flooded with water. A large amount of water was heavily running over the edge of the bathtub. Owing to the shocking scene, he remained standing there, unfocused for a while with his mouth wide open.

Then Ryu came to myself and thought he had to turn off the faucet. He walked into the warm water and swiftly turned it off. Gradually, he became calmer and began to analyze the situation, looking around the room. First, he had to cope with the hot water in the bathroom, especially around the white toilet stool. A drain was set up in the bathroom, so he had to guide as much water as possible into the waste pipe. When he checked the flow of water, it was swirling around and running into the pipe. However, the drain was not large enough to deal with such a large amount of water. Therefore, he threw a large bath towel around the stool to try to make it absorb more water. He used two large bath towels to stop water from flowing into the bedroom like a cascade. "One down! OK. What's next?" he thought. He encouraged himself to do something next. When he looked around the room, it was half covered with hot water. He found the water ran under the door outside of the room into the corridor, so he used hotel towels to stop it.

Vocabulary Check

英単語に合う意味を右の日本語から選び，(　　　) に記号を記入しなさい。

1 soak	(　　　　　)	a. 意識下の
2 faucet	(　　　　　)	b. 通路
3 roar	(　　　　　)	c. じめじめした
4 corridor	(　　　　　)	d. 滝
5 fatigued	(　　　　　)	e. 疲れて
6 subconscious	(　　　　　)	f. 水道
7 soggy	(　　　　　)	g. 浸す
8 drain	(　　　　　)	h. とどろく
9 cascade	(　　　　　)	i. 渦巻く
10 swirl	(　　　　　)	j. 排水溝

Listening Section　英文をよく聞いて，英語で答えよう。

1 ______________________________

2 ______________________________

3 ______________________________

4 ______________________________

Reading Comprehension

本文をよく読んで，次の問いに日本語で答えよう。

1　熱い湯を出す前に，龍は何をしましたか。

2　最悪のこと (That was his worst luck.) とは，何のことを言っていますか。

3　水の流れる音に目覚めたリュウは，浴室に行ってドアを開けたとき，そこで何を目にしましたか。

4　排水溝の水を確かめて，水が流れていたにもかかわらず，この事態になったのは何が原因と述べていますか。

Speaking Section

本文に合うように空所を埋めよう。但し，下線部には 2 語以上入る。その後，龍（Ryu）になったつもりで，パートナー（A）と対話をしてみよう。

<Part 1>

A: I heard you were staying at a nice hotel in Beijing. What did you first do at the hotel?

Ryu: I watched TV.

A: What kind of program did you see?

Ryu: Well… I watched, ______________________________, not dramas.

A: Ah, huh. Was there good news on TV?

Ryu: No. At that time, the male anchor on CNN was criticizing __________ _______________ on economic policy.

A: Oh, I see. Did you have a good night sleep?

Ryu: No.

A: Was there anything wrong with you?

Ryu: Honestly speaking, the ______________________________ in my room.

A: What? You let the bathtub (   )?

Ryu: Yes, that's right.

A: What made it happen, Ryu?

Ryu: I think that's because I ______________________________ from reading my paper and soundly asleep.

<Part 2>

A: Ryu, how long were you sleeping before you noticed the overflowing?

Ryu: I think I was sleeping for ______________________________.

A: ______________________________? But you may have slept longer.

Ryu: Yeah. Maybe, but I was at a loss about ______________________________ do next.

A: I know how you felt then. Did you do something to deal with it?

Ryu: Yes, of course. First, I walked on the soggy carpet and headed for the ( ) and then I ______________________________.

A: I think that's the first thing to do. You were cool and calm in the critical situation, weren't you?

Ryu: You can ______________________________again. I am in any situation.

A: You'd better not say such a thing, Ryu. You were a big ( ) at the hotel.

Ryu: I know. I know. Then, I threw a large ______________________________ around the toilet stool to try to make it __________________________.

A: That was an idea. But judging from your story, I assume the water was spreading into the ( ).

Ryu: That's right.

Grammar Section

ここでは接続詞の学習をしよう。接続詞には，次のようなものがある。副詞節では，譲歩（**though, although, even though** など），理由（**because, since, as**），条件（**if**），時（**when, before, after** など）がある。名詞節を導く接続詞には，**that** や **whether, if** がある。また，対等な内容や対立する内容をつなぐ接続詞では **and, but, so** などがある。具体的に本文中の例文を見てみよう。

When he looked around the room, it was half covered with hot water.
（部屋を見てみると，お湯で半ば水浸しであった。）

Since he felt like relaxing by himself there, he peeped into the bathtub and first washed it out using the shower.（そこでくつろぎたい気分だったので，浴槽を覗き込み，シャワーを使って水洗いをした。）

Before he knew it, he began to take a nap on the bed and shortly fell soundly asleep there.
（知らぬ間に，ベッドの上で転寝をし始め，ついに眠りについていた。）

It took a moment to focus on the noise **because** he was still half asleep.
（寝ぼけていたので，その音に耳を傾けるのに少し時間がかかった。）

Ryu came to myself **and** thought he had to turn off the faucet.

(龍は正気になって，蛇口を止めなくてはならないと思った。)

Arrange Words

(　　　　) 内の語を並べ替えて，正しい英文にしよう。

1 (Spain, make, wanted, though, trip, a, to, I, to), I needed to save more money to do it.

2 You have to make a specific plan (around, town, go, the, you, before, shopping)

3 Be sure to call on me (trouble, around, any, you, walking, if, have).

Writing Section

ここでは次の英語表現を学ぼう。

「理由」を示すお決まりの表現には，**because of** ～, **owing to** ～, **due to** ～「～の理由で」「～のために」がある。本文中の例文を見てみよう。

Owing to the shocking scene, he remained standing there.

(ショックな場面のせいで，彼はそこに突っ立ったままだった。)

次に，**deal with** ～, **cope with** ～で「～を対処する」「～を処理する」という意味を表す。例文で確認しよう。

He had to **cope with** the hot water in the bathroom.

(浴室のお湯を処理しなくてはならない。)

それでは，学習した英語表現を使って練習しよう。次の状況で英文を書いてみよう。

1 あなたは，友人と歓迎パーティの計画をしています。主賓の加藤氏が急に出張が入り，出席できなくなりました。そのことでパーティを延期しなければならないかもしれません。このことを The welcome party may…で始めて，上記の表現を用いて英語で表現してみよう。

2 あなたは，ある書類を誤って別の会社に郵送してしまいました。何とかその問題をすぐに対処するために上司に相談しなくてはなりません。このことを I have to consult...で始め deal with を使って，英語で表現してみよう。

Dictation Section

英語を聞いて書き取ってみよう。その英文の意味も書こう。

1 ________________________________

和訳（　　　　　　　　　　　　　　　　　　）

2 ________________________________

和訳（　　　　　　　　　　　　　　　　　　）

3 ________________________________

和訳（　　　　　　　　　　　　　　　　　　）

Unit 1 China Chapter 3 Hotel (2)

Ryu pushed his room door open quietly and looked down the corridor. It was past one a.m. and it was very tranquil around there. He found the hall floor had become dark blue for around 15 meters because of the running hot water. Judging from the spreading water, he easily expected that the water was slithering like a snake into some rooms beside his room and across from his.

Sheet on Soaked Carpet

Ryu thought, "Oh, no! What should I do? There's nothing I can do! What if I make a bath towel suck up the water here, as well?" He did it. Then, foam, looking like soap, emerged where he had wiped it. He supposed that it might have caused foam since the bath towel was not rinsed out enough. As a matter of fact, as he heard later, it had foamed because some synthetic detergent was left on the carpet in the corridor when it was last cleaned with a vacuum cleaner.

Ryu quit using the bath towel and went back to his room, pushing the door open slowly. He was flabbergasted to see the terrible situation while standing in front of the water-filled bathroom. He had already begun to think about the compensation for the damage. He thought, "It is flooded in this room, and the corridor has also become soggy... How much should I owe them?" Ryu had heard that someone else had run hot water onto the floor during his stay at an overseas hotel. This leaking water had annoyed people staying in the room below. However, he was so optimistic that he thought he would not get involved with such a case. Even so, he could not possibly hide this bad situation. He judged that he should get in touch with the hotel staff and honestly tell them about what had happened there. He wondered how the staff would feel about this terrible, unmanageable situation. Someone might have the feeling like this: "You good-for-nothing! How stupid Japanese people are!"

Getting ready to be criticized, Ryu ran downstairs directly instead of giving them a call. He got to the first floor while imagining a lot of harsh criticism and blunt attitudes from the hotel staff. He clearly explained to a female staff member what happened, but unexpectedly she did not show a curt attitude at all. Rather, she hurried to his room to grasp the described situation firsthand. She acted as if this was what she really wanted to do as a staff member.

The female staff member arrived at the spot where the floor was all covered with water. Ryu was awfully surprised to see her just deal with the problem calmly without being astounded at the awful scene. She also took appropriate measures to call people concerned and to ask for help to cope with this kind of problem.

A few minutes later, two male staff members came in, carrying a big vacuum cleaner. The machine was capable of sucking up water. They plugged it in and made the cleaner suck in water rapidly. The cleaner made a loud noise, but it had enough suction to do a good job in the room. It took about five minutes to finish vacuuming the room. When one of the staff members opened the lid of the vacuum cleaner, the tank was awash with dirty water. He poured the water into the drain of the bathroom.

Next, they rushed out of his room dragging the cleaner. They began to do the same job in the corridor, using this cleaner. Ryu felt so embarrassed to hear the cleaner making loud noises after one thirty a.m. Probably, many tourists had already fallen asleep in the wee hours of the morning. He was wondering what other vacationers were thinking about the noises coming from the corridor.

"What a nuisance! What are they doing around midnight like this?" Ryu imagined they would be thinking. But it took less than five minutes to get rid of the water in the corridor. After that, they went back to their normal job as if nothing had happened. He repeated to them, "I'm sorry. I'm sorry." At the same time he said, "Thank you very much." But it was no wonder they did not smile at him, since he troubled them a lot. What impressed him most at that time was that they didn't show him a wry face at all while they were doing the job. When Ryu apologized to them, they just uttered a simple word, "OK." Their facial expressions and the way of saying the word made him feel that they were trying to say, "That's all right. Never mind." Their relaxed attitudes relieved him from excessive anxiety, but at the same time he felt awfully sorry for his careless behavior. Is this what professionals show? He felt this case provided him with the opportunity that he should reflect on his halfhearted attitudes toward education as a professional teacher.

After the hotel staff left his room, Ryu drained some water out of the bathtub and took a bath. Looking vacantly at the ceiling, he was thinking about why this happened. Looking back, when he turned on the faucet, the following thoughts flitted through his mind, "Perhaps I might fall asleep on the bed, forgetting running hot water. I should not lie down on the bed watching TV."

His fear was realized! If only he had taken a shower. Or he wished he had not lain on the bed. **It is no use crying over spilt milk.** At that time, he was probably worn out because of doing his first presentation at an international conference.

Notes: You good-for-nothing! 役立たず！

Vocabulary Check

英単語に合う意味を右の日本語から選び，(　　　)に記号を記入しなさい。

1 rinse	(　　　　　)	a. 吸い込む
2 compensation	(　　　　　)	b. 放心したように
3 leakage	(　　　　　)	c. 休暇中の人
4 criticism	(　　　　　)	d. 滲出，漏出
5 curt	(　　　　　)	e. そっけない，ぶっきらぼうな
6 vacationer	(　　　　　)	f. すすぐ
7 vacantly	(　　　　　)	g. 口で言う
8 astound	(　　　　　)	h. 批判
9 suck	(　　　　　)	i. 驚愕させる
10 utter	(　　　　　)	j. 弁償

Listening Section　英文をよく聞いて，英語で答えよう。

1 ______________________________

2 ______________________________

3 ______________________________

4 ______________________________

Reading Comprehension

本文をよく読んで，次の問いに日本語で答えよう。

1　自分のしたことに対して，他の人がどう思うだろうと龍は想像していますか。

2　龍の部屋の状況を見て，ホテルの女性スタッフはどのような行動をしましたか。

3　ホテルスタッフが廊下を掃除し始めた時，龍がとてもばつの悪い思いをしたのは何故ですか。

4　水の処理をしてもらった後，このひどい出来事で龍はどんなことを考えさせられましたか。２つ書きなさい。

Speaking Section

本文に合うように空所を埋めよう。但し，下線部には 2 語以上入る。その後，龍（Ryu）になったつもりで，パートナー（A）と対話をしてみよう。

<Part 1>

A: Ryu, when you noticed it was more than you could handle, what did you do then?

Ryu: Well, I thought I should get in touch with the hotel staff and I went to the ______________________________.

A: Did you explain about the terrible situation?

Ryu: Yes. But I was very surprised she did not show me a ________________.

A: Really? What did she do then?

Ryu: She started to go to my room quickly to take a look at the (　　　　　　　).

A: Ah, huh.

Ryu: She saw the awful scene and ______________________________to people concerned to ask ______________________________.

A: Was she ______________________________ to deal with the problem?

Ryu: That she was.

A: Then, did other staff members come to your hotel room quickly?

Ryu: Yes. Two more staffers showed up __________________________ later.

A: How did they deal with the soggy room?

Ryu: They used a (　　　　　　　) cleaner to rapidly water.

A: Oh, really? I have never heard about such a (　　　　　　　) cleaner.

Ryu: Me, (　　　　　　　).

<Part 2>

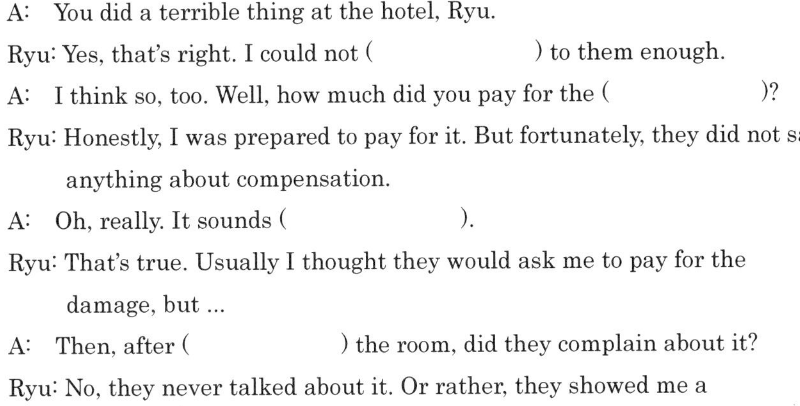

A: You did a terrible thing at the hotel, Ryu.

Ryu: Yes, that's right. I could not ( ) to them enough.

A: I think so, too. Well, how much did you pay for the ( )?

Ryu: Honestly, I was prepared to pay for it. But fortunately, they did not say anything about compensation.

A: Oh, really. It sounds ( ).

Ryu: That's true. Usually I thought they would ask me to pay for the damage, but ...

A: Then, after ( ) the room, did they complain about it?

Ryu: No, they never talked about it. Or rather, they showed me a ______________________.

A: Wow! That's incredible.

Ryu: I think so, too.

Grammar Section

このセクションでは関係代名詞 **what** の学習をしよう。他の関係代名詞と異なり，先行詞を含む関係代名詞である。したがって，**what** の前には先行詞が存在しない。 日本語では，通常「もの」「こと」の意味となる。本文中の例文で確認しよう。

(1) <u>What impressed him most at that time</u> was that they didn't show him a wry face at all.

（そのとき私が最も感動したのは，彼らが全くいやそうな顔を見せなかったことだ。）

(2) Is this <u>what professionals show</u>?

（これがプロの人が示すことなのであろうか。）

英文(1)の what は主語となる節（下線部）の中で使われており，一方英文(2)の what は補語となる節（下線部）の中で使われている。

Arrange Words

（　　　）内の語を並べ替えて，正しい英文にしよう。

1 (achieve, need, your, what, goal, most, to, you) is your constant efforts.

2 They misunderstood (situation, meant, that, what, in, I).

3 Look at the restaurant on the top of the mountain. Is (last, was, that, built, what, year)?

Writing Section

ここでは次の英語表現を学ぼう。

「驚き」を表す表現を見てみよう。主なものとして，**be surprised, be amazed, be astounded, be astonished, be startled** などがある。本文中の例文を見てみよう！

He was awfully surprised to see her just deal with the problem calmly.
（彼は，彼女が冷静に問題を処理するのを見てとても驚いた。）

このように，「驚き」を表す語の後に不定詞が続く場合と前置詞を伴う場合がある。前置詞の場合を例文で確認しよう！

I'm very surprised at his wonderful performance.
（彼の素晴らしい演技を見てとても驚いている。）

I was astounded at the sad news.
（その悲しい知らせを聞いて驚愕した。）

更に「驚き」を強調する表現として，本文中では **flabbergasted** が使われている。

He was flabbergasted to see the terrible situation.
（そのひどい状況を見て，あいた口がふさがらなかった。）

それでは，学習した英語表現を使って練習しよう。次の状況で英文を書いてみよう。

1 あなたは，(ゴルフが上手でないと思っていた) 友人がゴルフ選手権で優勝したのを聞いてとても驚いています。このことをI am very surprised ...で始めて，英語で表現してみよう。

2 あなたは，友人の突然の訃報を聞いてとても驚きました。このことをI was astounded ...で始めて，英語で表現してみよう。

Dictation Section

英語を聞いて書き取ってみよう。その英文の意味も書こう。

1 ________________________________

和訳(　　　　　　　　　　　　　　　　　　　　)

2 ________________________________

和訳(　　　　　　　　　　　　　　　　　　　　)

3 ________________________________

和訳(　　　　　　　　　　　　　　　　　　　　)

Unit 2 Hawaii

Unit 2 Hawaii　Chapter 4 Waikiki

After Ryu finished presenting his paper at the University of Hawaii, he was going to be back to the hotel just before three o'clock. He walked on campus toward the bus stop and was in time for the bus which was bound for Waikiki Beach. The bus was extremely crowded due to so many university students. Fortunately, he happened to find a seat on the bus and spent some time looking out of the window. Ryu was a little bit concerned about where to get off and he sometimes checked where he was, looking at the street names. After a while, he became relieved to see several buildings and scenery he remembered, such as the ABC stores. Ryu thought his bus would soon get to the bus stop where he should get off. He alighted at the shopping center across from a restaurant, and hurried to the hotel.

No sooner had he reached the hotel than he saw his wife, Kei, sitting back and relaxing on a sofa in the lobby. Ryu was really relieved to see her in Hawaii. He was extremely concerned about her departure from Japan

Waikiki Beach

and her arrival in Hawaii, as well. They just greeted each other, but without a hug. If they were local people in this situation, they would have hugged each other, saying hello or something.

"Hi, Kei. Aloha! Are you alright? You have arrived here safe and sound, haven't you? Where are our kids?" he asked.

"They are in their room. The hotel staff allowed us to enter the room, so our luggage was already in our rooms."

"That's good. Let's go upstairs."

Ryu went upstairs to the third floor and rushed into his children's hotel room. He found the children were fine. They greeted each other and Ryu expressed his honest feelings of relief to see them. Then they talked to each other about what to do for the rest of the day. The children wanted to swim in the sea along the coast of Waikiki Beach, so Ryu told them to change clothes there. They headed straight for the beach to swim in the sea.

The moment they got to the beach, his children were so impressed with the beautiful views that they shouted, "Wow! What a beautiful view! This is Waikiki, Hawaii! Wow! Wonderful! Beautiful! ..." Their exclamations went on and on while walking on the beach. They decided where to put their bags, and at once their kids went swimming in the beautiful sea. Ryu found so many people from various countries who were either swimming there or getting a suntan. Some people were surfing on the waves a little off the beach. His wife was video-recording the beautiful scenery and their kids' behavior in the sea. It looked as if they were not swimming but were just wading in the waves. However, they were 50 meters off the shore. Ryu and his wife were wondering if it would be all right to swim around there. They thought the sea would be shallow for a long distance from the shore.

After a while, their children went back to their spot on the beach. And then, instead of their children, Ryu and his wife went swimming. It seemed that rough waves sometimes made them almost drown. It never happened because they were just wading and swimming in the shallow sea. One time, a high wave struck them down. They sank in the sea completely above their heads. At that moment they started swimming to the shore. Ironically, Ryu later said to his wife, "What a good PE teacher! High waves made you show your skillful way of swimming, the dog paddle (*inu-kaki*)." She had a good laugh nodding at him.

They walked back to the hotel and changed clothes. They relaxed themselves for a while and went out for dinner. Ryu suggested to his family that they should eat out at a buffet-style restaurant. It was not only inexpensive but they could also eat whatever they liked and as much as they wanted. Therefore, everyone agreed to go there, following Ryu's recommendation. They occupied an open-air table and took turns getting their favorite food from the food bar. Ryu took potatoes, salad with tomatoes and lettuce, corn and fish, while his children and wife picked out meat, salad, chicken, and so on. After that, they ate melon, watermelon, pineapple and ice cream for dessert. While talking and eating at the table, the children took a great interest in birds walking around, aiming for leftovers that people left behind. They frequently talked about sparrow-like birds as well as different kinds of foods at the restaurant.

After dinner they stopped by an ABC store on their way back to the hotel, since his kids needed shoes for tomorrow's mountain-climbing outing. They bought the shoes which fit them, along with four bottles of water at the store.

Vocabulary Check

英単語に合う意味を右の日本語から選び，(　　　)に記号を記入しなさい。

1 extremely	(　　　　　)	a. 皮肉っぽく
2 relieve	(　　　　　)	b. 出発
3 alight	(　　　　　)	c. (水の中を) 歩く
4 departure	(　　　　　)	d. 極度に
5 hug	(　　　　　)	e. 安心させる
6 suntan	(　　　　　)	f. 抱く
7 exclamations	(　　　　　)	g. 日焼け
8 shallow	(　　　　　)	h. 浅い
9 wade	(　　　　　)	i. 降りる
10 ironically	(　　　　　)	j. 感嘆の声

Listening Section　英文をよく聞いて，英語で答えよう。

1 ______________________________

2 ______________________________

3 ______________________________

4 ______________________________

Reading Comprehension

本文をよく読んで，次の問いに日本語で答えよう。

1　大学からバスに乗った後，龍は何に不安を感じていましたか。

2　ホテルに着いたとき，龍は妻のどんな姿を目にしましたか。

3　泳いでいて高波に襲われた後，龍は妻に何と言いましたか。

4　レストランで子供たちが話していた話題は何でしたか。

Speaking Section

本文に合うように空所を埋めよう。但し，下線部には 2 語以上入る。その後，龍（Ryu）になったつもりで，パートナー（A）と対話をしてみよう。

<Part 1>

A: Ryu, did you go to Hawaii with your family?

Ryu: No. I had to attend a conference, so I left ( ) for Hawaii ahead of my family.

A: Uh, huh. Then did you ( ) to see them in Honolulu?

Ryu: Yes. I got on a bus at the ______________ to return to the hotel.

A: I think you had a nice view of Honolulu from the bus.

Ryu: I wanted to feel ( ) on the bus enjoying a good view, but …

A: Didn't you see the wonderful view from there?

Ryu: No, I didn't. The bus was ______________ with university students. But luckily I was able to ( ) on the bus.

A: How lucky you were!

Ryu: You can say that again.

<Part 2>

A: Ryu, did you swim in the sea along the coast of Waikiki Beach?

Ryu: Yes, of course. My children first ______________ there.

A: I see. Kids love swimming.

Ryu: As ______________ my children got to the beach, what do you think they did first?

A: Let me see … I don't know.

Ryu: Actually, they ( ) there.

A: Shouted?

Ryu: Yes. They were ______________ with the beautiful scene that they shouted. "Wow! What a ______________! This is

( )! Wow! Wonderful! ...”

A: Sounds like they had fun.

Ryu: I think they could not ( ) shouting there like that.

A: I feel like I understand how they felt.

Grammar Section

ここでは感嘆文と付加疑問文の学習をしよう。まず，感嘆文は**what**か**how**を使用する。本文の例文で確認しよう。

What a beautiful view!（なんて美しい景色だろう！）

Whatの場合は，「What a 形容詞+名詞（主語＋動詞）」のパターンで使用する。「How 形容詞/副詞　主語+動詞」で使用する。他の例文を見てみよう。

What a beautiful flower this is!

How beautiful this flower is!

「この花はなんてきれいなんだろう！」という意味であるが、語順に注意しよう。

次に，付加疑問文について説明しよう。例文から提示しよう。

He went to London, **didn’t he?** ↘（彼はロンドンへ行ったのですね。）

She is a PE teacher, **isn’t she?** ↗（彼女は体育の教師でしょ？）

You can’t come to the party tonight, **can you?** ↘ （パーティに来られないんですね。）

このように肯定文の場合は，否定の疑問文を作る形で語尾につける。否定文の場合は，肯定の疑問文の形を付加する。付加疑問文は，相手に同意を求めたり，確認したりする場合に使用する。通常，前者は上がり調子で，後者は下がり調子で言う。本文では，現在完了の付加疑問文が使用されている。

You have arrived here safe and sound, **haven’t you?** （無事にここに着いたんだね。）

Arrange Words

(　　　　) 内の語を並べ替えて，正しい英文にしよう。

1 His son shouted, "(is, a, view, What, this, wonderful)!"

2 She kept crying over and over, saying, "(accident, awful, the, was, How)!"

3 I (this, seen, never, like, impressive, an, have, film) before.

Writing Section

ここでは次の英語表現を学ぼう。

「**疑問詞+ to do**」の英語表現を学ぼう。例文で確認しよう。

Ryu was a little bit concerned about **where to get** off.
（龍はどこで降りたらよいのか少し不安であった。）

They talked to each other about **what to do** for the rest of the day.
（彼らは，その日の残りの時間何をしたらいいかお互いに話し合った。）

このように疑問詞には where, what, when などが使われ，「どこで（何を，いつ）～したらよいか，すべきか」の意味を表す。

それでは，学習した英語表現を使って練習しよう。次の状況で英文を書いてみよう。

1　あなたは，その町に初めてやって来ました。しかし，どこに行ったらよいのか途方にくれています。このことを I'm at a loss about で始めて，英語で表現してみよう。

2　あなたは，資格試験の勉強をしなくてはいけないのですが，まず何からやってよいのかさっぱりわかりません。このことを I don't know で始めて，英語で表現してみよう。

Dictation Section

英語を聞いて書き取ってみよう。その英文の意味も書こう。

1 ______________________________

和訳（ ）

2 ______________________________

和訳（ ）

3 ______________________________

和訳（ ）

Restaurant

Unit 2 Hawaii　Chapter 5 Diamond Head

Ryu looked over the magnificent view of the mountainous area and started his ascent of Diamond Head. The instant he started to climb the mountain with his family, he felt something strange around his abdominal region. He wondered if he should go to the toilet then while looking around for a bathroom close to him. Besides, he supposed there would be no toilets on the summit of the mountain. However, he ignored his natural urge of going to the toilet,

even though the facility was very close to him. At the same time, he was afraid there were no rolls of paper in the bathroom. That was the beginning of a most unpleasant experience.

Ryu was talking to his family about how long it would take to walk to the top and about what were the brown plants that looked withered. As they continued to climb up the winding paths, they gradually began to sweat. However, his wife, Kei, already had sweat a lot only halfway up the

Honolulu from Diamond Head

mountain. On the way up to the top, Kei sometimes video-recorded her children and the scenery, murmuring something like guiding the tour. Ryu also took photos of his family and beautiful views. Once in a while, their children stopped on the way and took some photos of the splendid views using their own cameras. Looking at people who were passing by or greeting them, Ryu hiked up toward the summit. The last time he visited Hawaii, he also ascended this unique-shaped mountain, Diamond Head. Therefore, he roughly remembered they faced steep slopes, a rest place and concrete stairs at the end of the climb. Just after they went into the dark tunnel and came out of the exit, they saw the narrow spiral stairs. Finally, they nearly reached the windy summit.

They started making the ascent of the mountain at 8:20 a.m. and almost reached the summit by 8:45 a.m. Ryu advised his children not to have their caps blown off by the wind. They were impressed by the magnificent views around them and continued to walk up to reach the summit. Just then, what a coincidence! Ryu saw Yoshi, a friend of his, and Yoshi's father at the mountain. They were trying to climb down from the top, while Ryu was almost at the summit of the mountain. First, he did not notice Yoshi but heard him call out Ryu's name. He looked up and said, "Oh, Yoshi. What a surprise! Did you climb to the summit already?"

"Yes. You advised me to climb Diamond Head early in the morning, didn't you?"

"Oh, yes, it gets hotter later on."

Just after exchanging greetings, they parted, but Ryu continued to talk to Yoshi from behind. "Yoshi, shall I take a photo of you?" Yoshi and his father looked back at Ryu and he took a picture of them. Then, Yoshi began to climb up higher again and proposed to Ryu that he should take a photo of Ryu's family. He was very happy to hear this from his friend on the summit and he was greatly thankful for his friend's kindness to take photos of them.

On the summit there were many climbers who enjoyed the nice views with a sense of contentment on their full faces. Ryu and his family had a good time looking at the wonderful views of the ocean, Honolulu and the mountainous area. That splendid scenery was a nice feast for their eyes. They spent about 30 minutes there, but something bad was happening inside Ryu's body—around his abdominal region and anus. He was afraid that he had to go to the toilet sooner rather than later.

Five minutes after they began to descend from the summit, Ryu started to wonder if he could endure the discomfort for another 20 minutes or so. The regular waves of uncomfortable feelings from the inside began to stimulate him hard. Each time it happened, he was obsessed with the psychological fear that he might not be able to tolerate it this time. Then again, the inner things were trying to come out, while he also encouraged himself, shouting in his mind again and again, "Ryu, you can do it! You can wait! Ryu, you are tested. Hang in there!" This time was also almost beyond the limit of his endurance. Just then, he happened to look at the right side of the road. The withered bushes spread all over and it seemed that he could hide himself to relieve himself there. The next moment he wondered what he should wipe himself with. It was not a good idea. Discarding this bad idea, he continued down in a hurry.

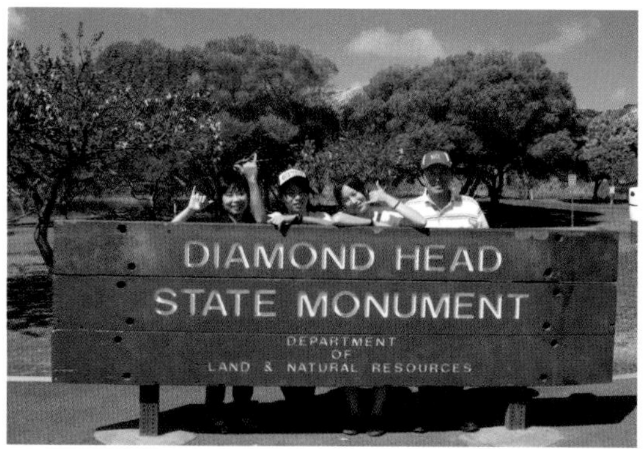

Diamond Head

Finally, they went past the rough path and got to a little wider road made of concrete. Ryu thought he just had to walk another 300 meters before he got to the bathroom. He encouraged himself again, silently saying to himself, "You can do it! You can endure it! Ryu, you can do it!" As the former American President, Mr. Obama, often said to the American people in the presidential election race, he reiterated, "Ryu! Yes, you can! Yes, you can!" At long last, he was there in the toilet at the foot of the mountain.

Twilight on Waikiki Beach

Vocabulary Check

英単語に合う意味を右の日本語から選び，（　　）に記号を記入しなさい。

1 magnificent	(　　　)	a. つぶやく
2 mountainous	(　　　)	b. 繰り返す
3 urge	(　　　)	c. 登る
4 wither	(　　　)	d. 満足（感）
5 murmur	(　　　)	e. 山の多い
6 ascend	(　　　)	f. 壮大な
7 coincidence	(　　　)	g. 駆り立てる力
8 part	(　　　)	h. 偶然
9 contentment	(　　　)	i. 別れる
10 reiterate	(　　　)	j. しおれる

Listening Section　英文をよく聞いて，英語で答えよう。

1 ______

2 ______

3 ______

4 ______

Reading Comprehension

本文をよく読んで，次の問いに日本語で答えよう。

1　山に登る前に，龍はふもとで何かを感じたのに無視しました。何を無視したのですか。

2　龍たちが曲がりくねった道を登って頂上に着くまでに，途中どんなところがありましたか。

3　龍は，頂上辺りで偶然誰に会いましたか。また，その時龍は彼らのために何をしましたか。

4 頂上に着いた登山者たちの様子はどうでしたか。

Speaking Section

本文に合うように空所を埋めよう。但し，下線部には 2 語以上入る。その後，龍（Ryu）になったつもりで，パートナー（A）と対話をしてみよう。

<Part 1>

A: Did you climb up the mountain, Ryu?

Ryu: Yes. That is the famous mountain which is popular among Japanese tourists.

A: I see. Did you have a good time there?

Ryu: Yes, but honestly, something bad happened to ____________________.

A: What happened, Ryu?

Ryu: I felt ______________________ around my abdominal region before climbing up.

A: Oh, no. Was it OK when you were climbing up?

Ryu: Yes. I did not care about it while climbing up. But after reaching the summit, I felt something bad around my abdominal region again.

A: Wow! Was there a (　　　　　　　) around there?

Ryu: No. That's why I had to (　　　　　　　) pain until I climbed down to the (　　　　　　　) of the mountain.

A: That's too (　　　　　　).

<Part 2>

A: Ryu, while climbing up, did you sweat some?

Ryu: Yes, of course. Especially, my wife who had a lot _________________ on the way up.

A: Oh! Does she sweat easily?

Ryu: I think so. But we had to keep walking along _____________________. My wife was taking charge of (　　　　　　　　　　) there.

A: Is she good at doing it?

Ryu: Anybody can do it, because the video camera is easy to use.

A: By the way, how was the view from the top?

Ryu: It was (   ). I was very ____________________ see the beautiful scenery.

A: Wow! I want to visit Hawaii, too.

Grammar Section

ここでは形容詞と副詞の学習をしよう。形容詞には限定用法と叙述用法がある。限定用法は，名詞を修飾して説明する用法であり，一方叙述用法は主語の性質や状態について述べる補語の形をとるものである。本文中の例文で確認しよう。

Ryu looked over the **magnificent** view of the **mountainous** area and started his ascent of Diamond Head.（龍は山岳地域の壮大な景色を見渡し，ダイヤモンドヘッドを登り始めた。）

He felt something **strange** around his abdominal region.（彼は下腹部あたりに異様なものを感じた。）

上記の 2 つの例文の中にある形容詞（太字）は，いずれも限定用法の形容詞である。例えば， **magnificent** view や **mountainous** area では，形容詞が後述される名詞 view と area をそれぞれ修飾して説明している。2 番目の例文中の something **strange** は，前述の something を修飾する後述形容詞となっている。

また，叙述用法の場合は，次の例文に見るように，形容詞（afraid）は主語（He）を説明する形となっている。

He was **afraid** that he had to go to the toilet sooner rather than later.

（彼は，すぐにでもトイレに行かなくてはならないのではないかと思った。）

次に，副詞の用法であるが，副詞は様態・程度・頻度・時・場所などを表す。「様態」を表す副詞は，どのようになされるかを示すもので，動詞の後におかれることが多い。「程度」を表す副詞には，almost, absolutely, completely, nearly, rather, quite などがある。「頻度」を表す副詞には，always, usually, often, sometimes, never などがあり，通常動詞の前におく。例文で確認しよう。

They **nearly** reached the windy summit.（彼らは，風の強い頂上にもう少し

で着くところだった。)

On the way to the top, Kei **sometimes** video-recorded her children and the scenery. (頂上へ行く途中，恵は時々子どもや景色のビデオを撮った。)

Arrange Words

(　　　) 内の語を並べ替えて，正しい英文にしよう。

1 Please come and see us (for, is, convenient, you, it, if).

2 I like Greece, but I (life, Athens, never, in, to, my, been, have).

3 (hot, like, to, you, something, would, drink) on such a cold day?

Writing Section

ここでは次の英語表現を学ぼう。

「have + 目的語（物）+ 過去分詞」「get + 目的語（物）+ 過去分詞」の形で「(物) を〜してもらう」「(物) を〜される」の意味を表す。本文中の例文で確認しよう。

Ryu advised his children not to **have their caps blown** off by the wind.
(龍は，子どもたちに風で帽子を飛ばされないように忠告した。)

それでは，学習した英語表現を使って練習しよう。次の状況で英文を書いてみよう。

1 あなたは，あなたの古くなった車が好きで乗っていましたが，帰りに故障してしまいました。そこで，そばにあるガソリンスタンドで修理してもらわなくてはなりません。このことを I have to で始めて，英語で表現してみよう。

2 あなたは，レストランの外にある傘立てに傘を置きました。でも，盗まれてしまうのではないかと心配しています。このことを I'm afraid I might で始めて，英語で表現してみよう。

Dictation Section

英語を聞いて書き取ってみよう。その英文の意味も書こう。

1 ______________________________

和訳（　　　　　　　　　　　　　　　　　　）

2 ______________________________

和訳（　　　　　　　　　　　　　　　　　　）

3 ______________________________

和訳（　　　　　　　　　　　　　　　　　　）

Unit 2 Hawaii　Chapter 6 Sightseeing

Ryu went back to the hotel at 10:30 a.m. He and his family relaxed for a while and then got ready for their next sightseeing spots: Monkey Pod Tree, Pearl Harbor, the Dole Plantation, and Sunset Beach. They were waiting for a van whose driver would show them around. At 11:20 the van arrived at their hotel to pick them up. Ryu seated himself in the front seat and his family members sat in the second row. Fortunately or unfortunately, he talked a lot to the driver in English, who asked Ryu to interpret what he said into Japanese. A Hawaiian of Japanese ancestry called Saito-san, was the driver-cum-guide of this tour. He was told to work for Japanese tourists as soon as possible, but he failed to show up at the office. Therefore, in lieu of him, Ryu was asked to interpret information about the first place they were going to visit, '*konoki-nannoki*'. The tree named like that was well-known among Japanese tourists because it has been shown in a Hitachi company's commercial on TV in Japan for over 20 years. A phrase in the lyrics is sung like this:

Monkey Pod Tree

"konoki nannoki kininaruki, mitakotomonai kidesukara mitakotomonai hanaga sakudeshou."(That is translated as: *What is this tree? It is the tree we are interested in. We have never seen the tree, so the flowers that we have never seen will bloom.)*

Ryu asked other people to take photos of them in front of the tree. He thought this was a place which only Japanese tourists would visit. Local people might be wondering why Japanese people are visiting such a common tree in this area. It *is* true. As a matter of fact, nobody visited there except for the Japanese.

Next, they visited Pearl Harbor, where the Japanese Navy attacked the fleets and bases with planes to start World War II against America. Ryu told his children the information on the history he knew about the surprise attack on Pearl Harbor. Like the monument in Okinawa, here was a list of war dead that were killed by the Japanese Air Force. He heard that some young Japanese people made noises or laughed there. They should not do that, since this is a revered place like the Peace Park in Hiroshima. If American people were making noises and looked happy at the Peace Park in Hiroshima, the Japanese there would surely get upset about it. This also holds true at Pearl Harbor. He told his children about the instructive story.

Then, they headed for the Dole Plantation. On the way to that sightseeing spot, they saw a vast wasteland around them. The taxi driver said, "There used to be pineapple fields as far as the eye could see. The fields completely changed last year because pineapples on Oahu Island became too expensive. At present, the tropical fruit is only planted on Maui Island." Ryu thought some cheaper pineapples would be imported from foreign countries such as the Philippines. At this Dole Plantation, local people were trying to manage their lives or to support tourism with reminders from the past. He was afraid the number of tourists would be gradually decreasing year by year. Visitors here didn't want to see things like antiques or to buy souvenirs based on this former prosperous industry.

However, Ryu thought that as long as there was Honolulu that attracted tourists, this plantation would be one of the local sightseeing spots. What the driver meant was that people related to local tourism would guide visitors to this plantation as one of the noted sightseeing spots.

They had dinner at the Cheesecake Factory, which was familiar to foreign tourists. It was introduced in many guidebooks, so Japanese visitors were sure to visit that popular restaurant. While having some favorite food, he intended to order a piece of cake for dessert. Unfortunately, he was already full. That was why he could not help but give up ordering the dessert.

After they had enough at that fancy restaurant, they stopped by one of the ABC stores and purchased good souvenirs for their friends and colleagues, such as key rings, straps for cell phones and Macadamia Nuts Chocolate.

……

Next morning, Ryu's family was supposed to leave Honolulu for Japan. His family had croissants and slices of pineapple and orange juice for breakfast in front of the reception desk. They needed cash to pay for taking a taxi to the airport. Although they managed to use the automatic teller machine (ATM) in the lobby, something like a receipt just came out of it. Ryu asked a hotel clerk at the front desk why he could not get cash from the ATM. He explained to Ryu that the ATM might not cover his JCB credit card. Therefore, as a result of checking the logos of credit card companies on the ATM machine, he noticed that there was no logo for his credit card company, JCB, on it.

Then he decided to withdraw cash at the bank closest to the hotel. They did not have enough time to go to another bank to get cash before their departure. Walking along the street, his wife proposed that they should obtain money from another bank close to the hotel or by shopping for something at an ABC store because they had accepted Japanese ten thousand-yen bills. Ryu agreed with her latter idea immediately and they hurried to the ABC store nearby to get US dollar cash. They bought cute straps and got green bucks there. What a relief!

Notes: Oahu Island オアフ島； Maui Island マウイ島

Vocabulary Check

英単語に合う意味を右の日本語から選び，(　　　)に記号を記入しなさい。

1 van	(　　　)	a.	未耕作の土地
2 lyrics	(　　　)	b.	観光業
3 monument	(　　　)	c.	思い出させるもの
4 upset	(　　　)	d.	骨董品
5 wasteland	(　　　)	e.	繁栄した
6 reminder	(　　　)	f.	歌詞
7 gradually	(　　　)	g.	記念碑
8 antique	(　　　)	h.	気分を害して
9 prosperous	(　　　)	i.	徐々に
10 tourism	(　　　)	j.	ワゴン車

Listening Section　英文をよく聞いて，英語で答えよう。

1 ______________________________

2 ______________________________

3 ______________________________

4 ______________________________

Reading Comprehension

本文をよく読んで，次の問いに日本語で答えよう。

1　ワゴン車の運転手は龍に何を頼みましたか。

2　Monkey Pod Tree が，日本人に人気がある理由は何ですか。

3　龍は子どもたちにパールハーバーで何を話しましたか。

4　このプランテーションは，どうやって生き延びているといっていますか。

Speaking Section

本文に合うように空所を埋めよう。但し，下線部には 2 語以上入る。その後，龍（Ryu）になったつもりで，パートナー（A）と対話をしてみよう。

<Part 1>

A: Ryu, did you do some sightseeing on Oahu Island?

Ryu: Yes. we visited ____________________, Pearl Harbor, and so on.

A: Did you rent a car there?

Ryu: No. We asked a ____________________ to show us those places.

A: I see. What's your favorite place?

Ryu: I liked Monkey Pod Tree. It's very famous among Japanese. Do you know about the tree?

A: No, I don't.

Ryu: Have you heard the ____________________ by Hitachi?

A: Umm... Hitachi? Well, I cannot remember it now.

Ryu: All right. I'll tell you the (   ). *Konoki nannoki kininaruki …*

A: Oh, I've heard the song.

Ryu: In that commercial you see a big tree, don't you? That is the Monkey Pod Tree.

A: Oh, I see.

<Part 2>

A: Did you go to the Dole Plantation, Ryu?

Ryu: Yes. I think it is a good sightseeing spot. But unfortunately, you cannot see vast pineapple fields.

A: Why is that?

Ryu: Pineapples are too (   ) to grow on Oahu Island and they are not (   ) there now.

A: That's too bad.

Ryu: However, you can enjoy yourself eating and drinking at souvenir shops and looking at various kinds of (   ) in a field beside the building.

A: I feel a little relieved to hear that. But I wonder how local people ________________________ at the plantation.

Ryu: I believe so. I think they are supporting local (   ) with ________________________ the past.

Grammar Section

ここでは時制（進行形）の学習をしよう。進行形は，時制によって様々な形で使用されている。現在進行形（am/is/are ＋～ing），過去進行形（was/were＋～ing），未来進行形（will be＋～ing）などがある。本文中の例文で確認しよう。

Local people **might be wondering** why Japanese **are visiting** such a common tree.

（地元の人々は，なぜ日本人があのようなありふれた木を訪れるのか不思議に思っているかもしれない。）

上記の英文では，「**might be wondering**」と「**are visiting**」の２つの進行形の形が使われている。前者は，助動詞のある進行形で，後者は現在進行形である。

他にも，現在完了進行形もある。これは動作を表す動詞の場合，過去から現在に至るまでの動作の進行を示すとき「have/has been～ing」の形で「(ずっと）～している」という意味を示す。

それを例文で見てみよう。

We **have been studying** English for 10 years. （私は10年間ずっと英語を勉強している。）

Arrange Words

（　　　）内の語を並べ替えて，正しい英文にしよう。

1 The (her, a lot of, was, with, woman, colleagues, drinking, alcohol) at the bar.

2 He (airport, be, at, for, will, the, me, waiting) because my plane is delayed.

3 The children (been, for, baseball, playing, three, have) hours today.

Writing Section

ここでは次の英語表現を学ぼう。

used to は現在と対比させて使用する表現である。したがって,「よく～した」「かつては～だった」という訳をする。本文の例文で確認しよう。

There **used to** be pineapple fields as far as the eye could see.

(かつては見渡す限り,パイナップル畑であった。)

「今はパイナップル畑ではない」という意味合いが,この英文に込められている。

一方,**would**(よく～した)の場合はよく副詞(often, sometimes など)を伴い,現在との対比はなく,単に過去の習慣を表す。

He **would** often play baseball.(彼はよく野球をしたものだ。)

それでは,学習した英語表現を使って練習しよう。次の状況で英文を書いてみよう。

1　かつて毎日タバコを吸っていたあなたの友人が,今は全く吸っていません。このことを上の語句を使って表現してみよう。

2　かつてあの空き地(vacant lot)には,ガソリンスタンドがありました。このことを There used to で始めて,英語で表現してみよう。

Dictation Section

英語を聞いて書き取ってみよう。その英文の意味も書こう。

1 ______________________________

和訳（　　　　　　　　　　　　　　　　）

2 ______________________________

和訳（　　　　　　　　　　　　　　　　）

3 ______________________________

和訳（　　　　　　　　　　　　　　　　）

Unit 3 Sri Lanka

Unit 3 Sri Lanka Chapter 7 Arrival in Colombo

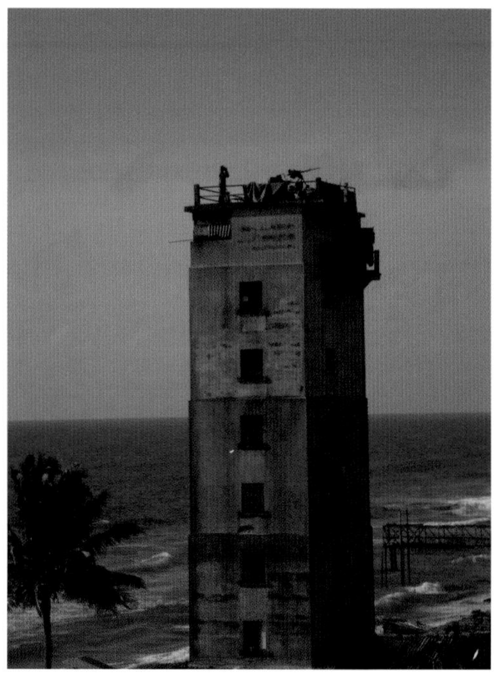

Army on the Top of the Tower

Ryu reached Kansai International Airport at 8:37 a.m. He hurried to the Cathay Pacific Counter and saw numerous passengers beside their suitcases standing in line. Finally, Ryu received his boarding pass at around 9:00 a.m. and embarked on the 10 o'clock flight to Colombo. Before leaving, he had bought in-flight slippers on the second floor of the airport terminal in order to have a comfortable flight in clean socks.

By way of Hong Kong and Singapore, Ryu arrived at Colombo Airport around midnight. It took more than 16 hours to reach Sri Lanka because of waiting times and transferring flights at each airport. Ranjan, a Sri Lankan friend of his, picked him up at the airport. Ryu was very happy to meet him there. They went forward through tight security by the army in Colombo because of the Tamil Tiger's possible attacks. Their car was stopped twice on the outskirts of Colombo by soldiers carrying a gun on their shoulders. They told Ranjan to show his identification card and asked him the reason for driving into the city. They were talking in their native tongue, Sinhalese, so Ryu could not make out their conversation at all. The Tamil Tigers have gradually weakened recently because the government has tried to control the whole country by gradually suffocating the guerrilla movement. Finally, they arrived at an exclusive hotel at past 1 a.m.

Ryu woke up at around 8:15 a.m. and had a leisurely breakfast with his friend, Yoshi. Ryu ate different kinds of fruits like papaya, pineapple, grapes and mango along with rice and spicy fish curry. Besides that, he had a slice of bread and flat bread like *nan* from India. While drinking red tea, Ryu talked a lot to Yoshi about their university jobs, sightseeing and their upcoming presentations in two days, as well. In front of them they had magnificent views of the vast ocean behind tall tropical trees. It was as if they were on an island with an everlasting summer, like Hawaii. They enjoyed the hearty breakfast, looking over the extensive sea. This was a time of supreme bliss. They needed to have this kind of sheer joy, especially since they had numerous hectic days at work. Otherwise, they may suffer from a serious ailment such as depression or they might even be driven to suicide. In order to avoid sinking into such a miserable state, people should have a relaxing time with their friends or family, and take action to enhance their self-esteem and self-confidence for living.

Ryu and Yoshi left their classy hotel for the downtown area around 10:30 a.m. They tried to take a traditional taxi peculiar to Sri Lanka which was called 'tuk tuk'. First, they were going to leave the luxurious white hotel and wander off, but they were not permitted to go out at that time. They heard that the roads were closed for another five minutes because the president of Sri Lanka was traveling to another place. They decided to get into a 'tuk tuk', which turned out to be the wrong choice. When they were trying to get into the three-wheeler, a slippery-looking guy went into their vehicle murmuring something. Though they did not know exactly why the stranger got in, Ryu thought the guy was one of the hotel staff who was going in the same direction as them. That ended up being wishful thinking. The guy was so aggressive. He started to explain to Ryu and Yoshi about his family, Japan, and Japanese people despite the fact that they did not ask him. It seemed that by continuing to say things related to Japan, this guy was aiming to alleviate their sense of danger about him. Ryu thought the guy tried to make them trust him while they were in the tuk tuk.

"My son, whose name is John Sebastian, is working at Colombo University and sometimes he teaches at a state-run university in Tokyo. His major is accounting."

Ryu suspected that he must be a liar. The guy might work at the hotel and he would probably be in charge of cleaning the lawn or something. However, Ryu had no idea who this odd man was working for in Colombo. There was a possibility that the guy targeted innocent tourists and deceived them to make his living. Instead of taking them to a bank, the driver and the odd guy drove Ryu and Yoshi to a jewelry shop. Ryu and Yoshi heard the Sri Lankans explain about many types of glittering jewels and then they insisted that Ryu and his friend purchase jewelry. Ryu had a bitter experience about jewel-shopping in Thailand, so he did not intend to buy anything at all. Even though the clerk insisted that they could cheaply buy precious jewelry, Ryu still didn't think so. When they got out of the tuk tuk, Yoshi paid 500 rupee to the driver.

At the jewelry shop they did not make a purchase and they tried to walk out alone without getting in the three-wheeler. However, this arrogant guy demanded that Ryu and Yoshi should take the traditional taxi because the place was a long way from a bank where they wanted to exchange money. The guy insisted that they should get in, so helplessly they succumbed to his demands and used the three-wheeler again. This was a big mistake. Ryu and Yoshi had to pay much more money when they tried to get off at the end of the trip. Correctly speaking, when the three-wheeler stopped in front of a certain huge building, Yoshi asked the driver how much they should pay. Ryu had no local currency, no rupee at that time, so Yoshi tried to hand a 1000 rupee bill to the driver and get the 300 rupee change. But then the strange guy demanded that they pay the 300 rupee as a tip. Though they negotiated for a couple of minutes or so, they relented and paid the 1000 rupee. Eventually, they turned out to be cheated by the chatterbox who forced himself into the three-wheeler with them at the start.

Vocabulary Check

英単語に合う意味を右の日本語から選び，(　　　)に記号を記入しなさい。

1 embark	(　　　)	a. つぶやく
2 identification	(　　　)	b. 高級な
3 outskirts	(　　　)	c. 抑圧する
4 suffocate	(　　　)	d. 乗り込む
5 exclusive	(　　　)	e. 身元確認
6 depression	(　　　)	f. 緩和する
7 self-esteem	(　　　)	g. 屈伏する
8 murmur	(　　　)	h. うつ病
9 alleviate	(　　　)	i. 郊外
10 succumb	(　　　)	j. 自尊心

Listening Section　英文をよく聞いて，英語で答えよう。

1 ____________________

2 ____________________

3 ____________________

4 ____________________

Reading Comprehension

本文をよく読んで，次の問いに日本語で答えよう。

1　タミールタイガーは，何故最近弱体化してきたのですか。

2　龍が「至福の時」と言っているのは，何のことですか。

3　乗り込んできた見知らぬ人は，龍たちを安心させるためにどうしましたか。

4　宝石を購入せず，歩こうとしていた龍たちを引き止めた傲慢なスリランカ人は，なぜ再度乗るように要求したのですか。

Speaking Section

本文に合うように空所を埋めよう。但し，下線部には 2 語以上入る。その後，龍（Ryu）になったつもりで，パートナー（A）と対話をしてみよう。

<Part 1>

A: Ryu, did you go to Sri Lanka?

Ryu: Yes. I left ( ) International Airport for ( ).

A: What airline did you use to go there?

Ryu: I used ____________________ Airline.

A: Did you fly directly to Sri Lanka?

Ryu: No, unfortunately I had to go there by way of ( ) and ( ).

A: Wow! It ( ) have been a long time to get there.

Ryu: That's true. Also, after I got there, I had a lot of trouble.

A: What was it?

Ryu: First, it took a long time to get into the city, since they had ________________ there.

A: Why was that?

Ryu: I think it was because of the _______________________ possible attacks.

<Part 2>

A: After arrival, you must have been very tired from the long trip.

Ryu: Of course. But we did not have time to take a nap the next morning.

A: You mean, you _________________ early in the morning?

Ryu: Yes. Also, I had a big ( ) with my friend.

A: What did you eat then?

Ryu: I ate different kinds of ( ), such as papaya, ( ), grapes and ( ) along with rice and spicy ____________________.

A: Wow! I have never eaten papaya and mango.

Ryu: You should visit the country to eat many kinds of fruits. Apart from eating fruits, we had a good time and a bad time, as well.

A: Bad time? What happened to you there?

Ryu: We took a (   ) instead of a normal taxi. Then a strange guy showed us a (   ) shop, though we did not want to buy it.

A: What? He really was a strange guy, wasn't he?

Ryu: I think so, too. But we were (   ) by that guy. I mean, finally we had to pay 300 rupee as a (   ), as well.

A: That's too bad.

Grammar Section

ここでは助動詞の学習をしよう。助動詞には，can, will, may, must, should, ought to などがある。動詞を補助して，意味を加える役目を果たす。また，could, would, might などは少し距離を置いた意味合いを表す。例文で助動詞の意味を確認しよう。

They **may** suffer a serious ailment such as depression.
（彼らは，うつ病のような深刻な病気にかかるかもしれない。）

People **should** have a relaxing time with their friends or family.
（人は友人や家族とリラックスした時間をもつべきだ。）

また，could have 過去分詞（～できたのに），should have 過去分詞（～すべきだったのに），must have 過去分詞（～したに違いない），cannot have 過去分詞（～したはずがない），may have 過去分詞（～したかもしれない）などの表現は，そのことが実現しなかった（あるいは推量の）意味合いを出す。

He **must have been** late for class this morning.
（彼は，今朝授業に遅れたに違いない。）

You **should have gone** there instead of your friend.
（あなたは，友人の代わりにそこへ行くべきだったのに。）

Arrange Words

（　　　）内の語を並べ替えて，正しい英文にしよう。

1 It is so hot today. (open, you, you, windows, would, the, behind)?

2 It is ten thirty. (meeting, late, be, faculty, may, for, the, we).

3 He didn't say anything to his boss about his mistake. He (boss, apologized, his, to, for, have, should) his mistake.

Writing Section

ここでは次の英語表現を学ぼう。

insist（主張する/要求する）という動詞の使い方を学習しよう。この動詞は次のような使い方をする。

(1) insist that S'+(should) V'

(2) insist on (someone) doing / insist on (something)

その使用法を例文で確認しよう。

They insisted that Ryu and Yoshi purchase jewelry.

（彼らは龍と芳に宝石を買うように主張した。）

他にも **demand**（要求する）や **propose**，**suggest**（提案する）などの動詞も，動詞の後に that 節を伴う。本文中の例文で見てみよう。

The strange guy demanded that they pay the 300 rupee as a tip.

（その見知らぬ男は，彼らにチップとして 300 ルピー払うよう要求した。）

それでは，学習した英語表現を使って練習しよう。次の状況で英文を書いてみよう。

1　あなたは，今会社のセールスで飛び回っています。社長から直々に（in person）全社員に，今月新しい商品を一人最低 20 ずつ販売するように強く要求されました。このことを demand を使って，英語で表現してみよう。

2　この夏キャンプを計画しています。奈津子がキャンプなら蓼科（たてしな）がいいと主張しています。このことを insist を使って，英語で表現してみよう。

Dictation Section

英語を聞いて書き取ってみよう。その英文の意味も書こう。

1 ______________________________

和訳（　　　　　　　　　　　　　　　　　　）

2 ______________________________

和訳（　　　　　　　　　　　　　　　　　　）

3 ______________________________

和訳（　　　　　　　　　　　　　　　　　　）

Unit 3 Sri Lanka Chapter 8 Colombo

Ryu was walking toward the station in an excited state with his friend, Yoshi. On the way to the nearest local station, they made up their mind to drop by a small bookstore on the main street which carried a wide variety of famous novels and traditional fairy tales, such as Christmas Carol and Huckleberry Finn. While Ryu looked through the titles on the bookshelves, he happened to see the writings compiled by Dale Carnegie, a prominent speech and presentation expert. The books were reasonably priced. One volume cost no more than 350 rupee, about 400 yen. Ryu thought that one publication written by this well-known author would cost at least 1500 yen in Japan. However, he suspected that perhaps the author's works might be pirated editions that were manufactured in a certain Asian country. However, Ryu looked through the copies to ensure they were genuine articles and, as a result, he bought four distinguished writings by Dale Carnegie.

Kollupitiya Railway Station

Ryu and Yoshi had an original plan to head for Colombo by train, so they were looking for the nearest station. Whenever they asked for the direction, local passers-by, pointing in a certain direction, gave them almost the same response: "It's over there. It's about 100 meters." Each time they asked a local person, they trusted that person and walked in the direction the passer-by pointed to. However, they found it hard to get to the destination and decided to find the station by themselves. Before he knew it, Ryu talked to himself ironically, "Ah! Nearest (station) is really NEAR!" At that moment, it chanced that the sign, 'Station Road' came into view all of a sudden. "Oh, here!" he thought. But Ryu did not see any building like a train station as far as he could see. When he wondered where the station would be located, his eyes fell on the sign 'Station Road.' While they were walking further on a very dusty road, Ryu found a woman carrying a big bamboo bag on her head and asked her about the station again.

"It's over there," she said, pointing at a certain sooty, dirty and antiquated building behind them. They looked back toward the direction she indicated. They saw the name of the station on the board, written in both Sinhalese and English. "Oh, we are there," he thought. They had already been very close to the entrance of the station. No wonder they could not find the building easily. It did not look like the train station they had imagined. Also, they had the fixed idea that the railroad station reminded them of regular tracks and a traditional entrance. Of course there were railway tracks from station to station, but the buildings along the coast obstructed their field of vision. The station was called Kollupitiya Railway Station, where they paid 10 rupee for the ticket to Colombo Fort Station. The wooden station was reminiscent of the good old days in Japan.

Ryu and Yoshi were standing on the sooty platform, looking unfocusedly over long railroad tracks. Beyond the platform was the vast ocean where rough waves were rolling in across the shore. Then Ryu talked to military-dressed workers who were mainly watching passengers there.

They did not seem to be good at speaking English, so Ryu could barely communicate with them. He relied on using body language, paraphrasing and speaking only simple, basic words, not whole sentences. On the other hand, his friend was enjoying conversation with two local naïve teenage girls.

The train was so old and dirty that they were reminded of the old recovery days after World War II in Japan. The floor was made of wood and no doors were on the car. Local passengers were getting on and off without worrying about not having doors on each car. However, everyone looked very happy and was talking merrily together on the train. From Ryu's point of view, the scene did not look clean or good, but the local people seemed very kind and pure in heart.

They walked around one of the districts in Colombo, Pettah, after getting off the train at Colombo Fort Station. Ryu went to the bathroom, but it was extremely dirty and stinky. Therefore, he had to stop breathing in there. Ryu almost threw up because of the offensive smell that greeted his nostrils. While walking through the narrow streets in the Pettah area, they sometimes visited bookstores or looked over the different kinds of food stands. They were so weary and frustrated because they had to weave their way through an enormous crowd and a traffic jam. A whole slew of cars and three-wheelers were running along the narrow streets, frequently honking their horns. At the same time, local people were slipping straight through the traffic as if they did not care about the busy street. Ryu and Yoshi were very nervous and feeling how risky it was when they were trying to cross the street. So they could not act like local people.

Ryu and Yoshi were waiting for their train at Colombo Fort Station to go back to their exclusive hotel. They talked to a kind, gentle man about their jobs and family, while waiting on platform number 5. He was a carpenter who built houses or produced furniture, and so on. Next to this guy were his family members waiting for the same train. Ryu heard that he sometimes traveled to Saudi Arabia and Oman for his work. While Ryu was talking to him, he wondered about their train not pulling in. The train was delayed for about one hour. They said it was quite common for the train to be delayed, so the locals did not seem to be irritated about it at all. Ryu felt as if he were advised as follows: Don't be in a panic. The train will come in soon. **Everything comes to those who wait.** That saying is a way of living in Sri Lanka.

Notes: Kollupitiya Railway Station コッルピティヤ駅； Pettah ペター

Vocabulary Check

英単語に合う意味を右の日本語から選び，(　　)に記号を記入しなさい。

1 distinguished	(　　　)	a. 純朴な
2 compile	(　　　)	b. 思い起こさせる
3 publication	(　　　)	c. 際立って優れた
4 reminiscent	(　　　)	d. 疲れ果てた
5 paraphrase	(　　　)	e. 古風な
6 naïve	(　　　)	f. 出版物
7 antiquated	(　　　)	g. 言い換える
8 sooty	(　　　)	h. すすけた
9 Sinhalese	(　　　)	i. シンハラ語
10 weary	(　　　)	j. まとめる，編集する

Listening Section　英文をよく聞いて，英語で答えよう。

1 ____________________

2 ____________________

3 ____________________

4 ____________________

Reading Comprehension

本文をよく読んで，次の問いに日本語で答えよう。

1　何故，龍は手ごろな値段の本をすぐに購入しなかったのですか。

2　龍は駅で軍人風の人と話した時，どのようにして彼はコミュニケーションをとりましたか。

3　龍が乗った列車は，どのような列車でしたか。

4　帰りのプラットホームで電車を待っていて，列車が来なかったときの龍は，どんなことを感じていましたか。

Speaking Section

本文に合うように空所を埋めよう。但し，下線部には 2 語以上入る。その後，龍（Ryu）になったつもりで，パートナー（A）と対話をしてみよう。

<Part 1>

A: Did you visit Sri Lanka, Ryu?

Ryu: Yes, I had a good time staying there with my friend, (　　　　　).

A: That was good. Where in Sri Lanka did you go?

Ryu: We visited Colombo, but we had a lot of ________________ on the train.

A: What happened to you?

Ryu: It was not easy to find the ________________.

A: How did you find it?

Ryu: We asked some ________________ for directions, but they gave the ________________ to us.

A: What do you mean by that?

Ryu: They surely (　　　　　) in a certain direction and said, "It's ____________."

A: Sounds interesting.

Ryu: I don't think so. Actually, we needed a lot of (　　　　　) to find the destination.

A: Finally, how did you find it?

Ryu: The last person we asked for the place pointed directly at the train station.

A: Oh, that's a relief, I'm sure.

<Part 2>

A: Ryu, did you buy anything there?

Ryu: Yes, I bought ________________________ written by ____________.

A: Who is he?

Ryu: He was a prominent speech and presentation (   ) in the US.

A: Oh, I see. I didn't know about him.

Ryu: You should read his books, because they are very (   ) when you try to give a good (   ) and lead a better life.

A: OK. Thank you for your advice. How much did you pay for four books?

Ryu: I paid only (   ) rupee. This is equal to about (   ) yen.

A: Wow! That's reasonable. Did you have any bad experiences there?

Ryu: The toilet at Colombo Fort Station was terrible.

A: How so?

Ryu: It was extremely (   ) and (   ).

A: That's too bad.

Grammar Section

ここでは分詞の学習をしよう。分詞には現在分詞と過去分詞がある。現在分詞の場合は，通常「～している」，過去分詞の場合は「～される，されている」という日本語で意味をとる。本文の例を参考にして意味の確認をしていこう。

現在分詞の場合：

Ryu found a woman **carrying** a big bamboo bag on her head.

（龍は，頭の上に大きな竹製の袋をのせた女性を見つけた。）

この英文の現在分詞は，前の語を修飾している。次に過去分詞の場合をみてみよう。

過去分詞の場合：

Ryu bought four distinguished writings **compiled** by Dale Carnegie

（龍は，デール・カーネギーによってまとめられた 4 冊の優れた著作本を買った。）

この英文の過去分詞は，前の語を修飾している。他に分詞として重要な表現は分詞構文である。分詞構文は，原則「～ing」の形を使用して，理由・条件・時・譲歩・付帯状況などを表す。

例）**Speaking of** sushi, his favorite kind is sea urchin.

（寿司といえば，彼の大好物はウニだね。）

上記の分詞構文は，慣用的な分詞構文である。「**Speaking of** ～」（～についていえば）で覚えておくとよい。主な慣用的な分詞構文を列挙しておく。

Considering（～を考慮すると）, **Frankly speaking**（率直に言えば）, **Strictly speaking**（厳密にいえば）, **Talking of**（～について言えば）, **Judging from**（～から判断すると）

Arrange Words

（　　　）内の語を並べ替えて、正しい英文にしよう。

1 We find so many construction (a, condominium, build, working, to, new, employees).

2 The teacher instructed students to do the (classroom, around, walking, the, task, while).

3 The mother was working beside (kitchen, dolls, child, with, in, playing, her, the).

Writing Section

ここでは次の英語表現を学ぼう。

「**happen to** ～」「**It (so) happens that** S'＋V'」「**It chances that** S'＋V'」は，日本語で「たまたま～する」という意味に相当する。本文中の例文で，この表現を確認しよう。

He **happened to** see the writings compiled by Dale Carnegie.

（彼は，たまたまデール・カーネギーによってまとめられた著書を目にした。）

It chanced that the sign came into view all of a sudden.

（偶然，突如としてその看板が彼らの目に入った。）

それでは，学習した英語表現を使って練習しよう。次の状況で英文を書いてみよう。

1　あなたは，帰宅途中立ち寄った本屋で，偶然あなたの先生に会いました。このことを It happened that で始めて，英語で表現してみよう。

2　今日の予定について，友人と話し合っています。あなたは，今日はたまたま空いています。このことを I で始めて，英語で表現してみよう。

Dictation Section

英語を聞いて書き取ってみよう。その英文の意味も書こう。

1 ____

和訳（　　　　　　　　　　　　　　　　　　　　　　　　）

2 ____

和訳（　　　　　　　　　　　　　　　　　　　　　　　　）

3 ____

和訳（　　　　　　　　　　　　　　　　　　　　　　　　）

Unit 3 Sri Lanka Chapter 9 Hospital

At a dinner party Ryu selected his favorite foods from among the dishes, such as crab, tuna, and kingfish. Without knowing that a nightmare would occur to him that night, he had a good time chatting with others and eating various kinds of foods, fruits and fish. Two hours later they finished the enjoyable party and went back to their own rooms. Ryu took a shower and slept like a log due to fatigue after the presentation and feeling tipsy. Late at night, all at once, he felt nauseated and had an agonizing pain in his stomach and intestines. He jumped out of the bed, rushed straight to the bathroom, and had loose stools again and again throughout the night. At the same time he vomited there several times every hour all night long.

Next morning his friend Ranjan noticed Ryu's pale diseased condition and took him to the medical department at the university. The doctor asked him to sit and to explain what was wrong. Ryu talked weakly

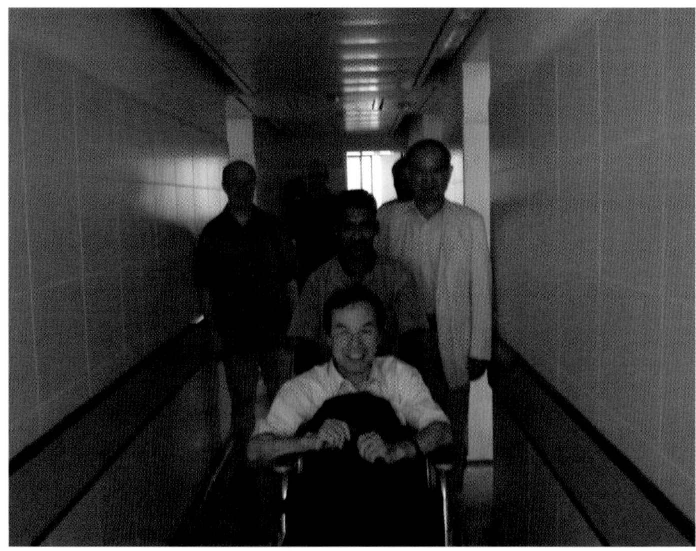

Ryu in the Wheelchair

about the miserable experience he had last night. Then the doctor told Ryu to lift his tongue and he took his temperature. He was a little bewildered to hear the doctor. "What? Move up my tongue?" Ryu thought, "It depends on the country how to take the temperature. In Sri Lanka the doctor puts a thermometer under a patient's tongue to take a temperature." After a while the doctor said, "38.5 degrees. You have a fever." Then Ryu was trying to say something more, but the next moment, all of a sudden, he felt uneasy. He feared he might vomit on the spot in front of the doctor, so he showed the easy-to-understand gesture of throwing up to others. Ranjan noticed it instantly and pointed at the washstand for hand-washing. No sooner had Ryu seen it than he rushed there and started vomiting four times, even though he threw up so many times the night before. He was sure that there would be no gastric contents in his stomach because of last night's sufferings and tribulations. Unbelievably, that was not true.

After walking unsteadily back to the seat in front of the doctor, he was asked about his allergies to medicine and so on. Then he took some pills to cure his stomachache and some oral rehydration salts to get over dehydration. He was told to lie down and to rest on a bed for a while. Ryu fell asleep on the bed for about two hours owing to a lack of sleep and fatigue. Ranjan woke him up at around 12 o'clock and asked him if he wanted to go to a general hospital outside the university. The doctor recommended that Ryu visit a doctor at a hospital, because he still had a fever and symptoms of dehydration due to frequent vomiting. Ryu agreed and Ranjan drove him to the suggested hospital.

When they got to their destination, they saw numerous patients who were sitting or standing outside the building. Though Ryu thought he would have to stand in line, Ranjan passed through the crowd and went straight to a female doctor. In all likelihood he called the hospital and talked to them about Ryu's condition in advance. One of the female doctors dressed in white clothes, instructed him to sit beside the doctor's desk. Then she began to whisper to a male doctor. She asked Ryu what seemed to be the problem, just as the doctor had at the university. He told her about a series of medical problems last night and this morning as well. She asked him if he had allergies to medicine or food, along with what diseases he had contracted throughout his lifetime. Then the female doctor took his blood pressure and temperature, putting a thermometer under his tongue in the Sri Lankan way. Eventually, they decided to feed Ryu intravenously in a private room.

Ryu was put in a wheelchair because he could not walk straight in a natural way. A male employee, working at the hospital, pushed the wheelchair to one of the rooms on the third floor in an annex building. He had a little, strange feeling of being a real patient. Actually, Ryu felt being looked down on by local people at the medical building, including outpatients, because he had priority treatment. They passed through a narrow corridor and arrived at the end rooms of the floor. On the left side of the corridor was a room where Ryu thought he would be put. It had a TV set and a refrigerator, and he was allowed to watch TV if he wanted to. Another doctor came to his room with a nurse and asked, “Are you OK? Are you hungry?” Ryu answered, “A little. I don’t have much of an appetite.” Then she brought a glass of apple juice and some snacks for him.

Ten or fifteen minutes later, a male nurse came in and asked so many questions. However, they were not so clear to him because the nurse spoke English with a strong accent of his native tongue, Sinhalese. Ryu understood most of the nurse’s words and managed to answer his questions like this, using technical terms.

“Have you ever had asthma? Did you ever have diabetes, cholera, or kidney disease?” The instant Ryu responded in the negative about all the diseases he mentioned, the nurse asked him, “Have you ever had a cough?” Ryu was a little confused because that reminded him of coughing when people had a cold. After a moment, he guessed it would be ‘whooping cough’

(*hyakunitizeki* in Japanese), so he soon answered, "No, I have never had a cough."

Sometime later, Ryu was put on an intravenous (IV) drip for an hour, or so. Around the time the IV drip finished, another female nurse came to his room and offered him the statement of the total charges. He thought, "About 6500 rupee, which corresponds to about 7500 yen. That's not so bad when you think about the treatment." He paid the money for it in person, there and then. As he was sitting in the wheelchair, he went through the corridors and finally exited out of the hospital.

ASIRI HOSPITALS LTD.
181 Kirula Road, Colombo 5.

DIAGNOSIS CARD

BHT No 173773
RM No 308

Name : MR. Koji Ueoishi
D. O. B : 51Y
Date of Admission : 19/09/08
Address : NO 139/10/A Ruwan Rd Pelanwatta, Pannipitiya
Dr. : S. Mendis
Date of Discharge : 19-09-2008

Dr. B. Sriyantha Mendis
MD FRCP
CONSULTANT PHYSICIAN

Acute Gastroenteritis

Diagnosis Card

Vocabulary Check

英単語に合う意味を右の日本語から選び，(　　　) に記号を記入しなさい。

1 bewildered	(　　　　　　)	a.	嘔吐する
2 thermometer	(　　　　　　)	b.	静脈内に
3 vomit	(　　　　　　)	c.	脱水症状
4 gastric	(　　　　　　)	d.	外来患者
5 intravenously	(　　　　　　)	e.	体温計
6 dehydration	(　　　　　　)	f.	胃の
7 diabetes	(　　　　　　)	g.	糖尿病
8 asthma	(　　　　　　)	h.	当惑する
9 fatigue	(　　　　　　)	i.	喘息
10 outpatient	(　　　　　　)	j.	疲労

Listening Section　英文をよく聞いて，英語で答えよう。

1 ______________________________

2 ______________________________

3 ______________________________

4 ______________________________

Reading Comprehension

本文をよく読んで，次の問いに日本語で答えよう。

1　医学部の医者による診察時に，その部屋で龍に何が起こりましたか。詳しく述べなさい。

2　何故，龍は自然な形でまっすぐ歩くことができなかったのですか。

3　病院に着いた龍は，多くの外来患者の後に並んで順番を待つ必要がありませんでした。それは何故ですか。

4 龍は，看護師の咳に関する質問に何故困惑したのですか。また，結局龍は，そのことをどのように理解したのですか。

Speaking Section

本文に合うように空所を埋めよう。但し，下線部には 2 語以上入る。その後，龍（Ryu）になったつもりで，パートナー（A）と対話をしてみよう。

<Part 1>

A: I heard you became sick in Colombo.

Ryu: That's right. I had a pain in my (　　　　　　) and (　　　　　　) after the dinner party.

A: What made it happen?

Ryu: Probably it was because of the food I ate at the party.

A: What did you eat there?

Ryu: I had some (　　　　　　) such as tuna and crab.

A: Did you see a doctor?

Ryu: Yes. First, my friend Ranjan was kind enough to take me to a doctor at the (　　　　　　) department, where strangely enough, the doctor told me to ______________________________.

A: What ? What was that for?

Ryu: He tried to take my (　　　　　　) by doing that. It sounds a little strange for us, but you know, the saying (　　　　　　), "When in (　　　　　　), do as the (　　　　　　) do."

A: That's true.

<Part 2>

A: After going to the doctor at the university, did you (　　　　　　) from your sickness?

Ryu: Unfortunately, no. The doctor recommended that I go to another (　　　　　　), so Ranjan took me there.

A: I see.

Ryu: Then I was taken to a (   ) room in a (   ).

A: Oh, no. Did you have a (   ) disease?

Ryu: I don't think so. But I had (   ) at that time, so the doctor seemed to be a little concerned about me.

A: So, you didn't have an (   ), did you?

Ryu: That's right. But even so, a nurse brought a glass of ____________________ and some (   ) for me.

A: That's very kind of her. After that, what kind of (   ) did you get in the room?

Ryu: I got an ____________________ there for an hour or so.

A: Ah, huh. Was it very effective for you ?

Ryu: Yes, I think it was.

Grammar Section

ここでは話法の学習をしよう。話法には直接話法と間接話法がある。直接話法は，話し手が直接言った言葉（"）で，その言葉が伝達される。一方，間接話法は，間接的に別の人に伝達する時に使用される。肯定文・疑問文・命令文など文章の型によってパターンが異なる。常に時制の一致・人称の転換等に注意しよう。本文中の英文で，それぞれのパターンを見てみよう。

＜肯定文＞

間接話法の場合，that 節でつなぐ。

Ryu said, "I don't have much of an appetite."（直接話法）

Ryu said that he didn't have much of an appetite.（間接話法）

＜疑問文＞

Yes, No で答える疑問文の間接話法の場合，if か whether でつなぐ。

疑問詞のある疑問文の場合は「ask 人」の後に「疑問詞＋S' V'」の形でつなぐ。

She asked him, "Do you have any allergies to medicine or food?"（直接話法）

She asked him if he had some allergies to medicine or food.（間接話法）

＜命令文（依頼文）＞

命令文の間接話法の場合は，「tell 人 to 不定詞」のパターンでつなぐ。丁寧な依頼の場合は，「ask 人 to 不定詞」で間接話法にする。忠告などの場合は advise を使用する。

The doctor said to Ryu, “Lift your tongue.”（直接話法）

The doctor told Ryu to lift his tongue.（間接話法）

Arrange Words

(　　　　) 内の語を並べ替えて，正しい英文にしよう。

1 He asked me (mall, shopping, wanted, at, I, to, the, whether, go) or not.

2 I told him (behave, dinner, himself, should, party, at, he, that, the).

3 She asked her (that, home, possible, come, to, soon, as, mother, as) evening.

Writing Section

ここでは次の英語表現を学ぼう。

本文では，**look** を用いた **look down on**（～を見下ろす）が使われている。他にも look を用いた表現には，次のようなものがある。**look up to**（尊敬する），**look into**（調べる），**look over**（ざっと見る），**look high and low**（くまなく探す）など数多くある。本文では，次の英文で使われている。

Actually, he felt being **looked down on** by local people at the medical building.

（実際，彼は医療棟で地元の人に見下ろされていると感じた。）

それでは，学習した英語表現を使って練習しよう。次の状況で英文を書いてみよう。

1 あなたは，中学校で英語を教えてもらったとても尊敬する恩師，迫田先生に偶然本屋で会いました。このことを帰宅して家族に話しています。これを I happened to...で始めて，英語で表現してみよう。

2 あなたは，「英文学」の授業でレポートを提出しなくてはいけません。そのために図書館の文献から Shakespeare について書かれている文書を調べる必要があります。このことを I have to...で始めて，英語で表現してみよう。

Dictation Section

英語を聞いて書き取ってみよう。その英文の意味も書こう。

1 ________________________________

和訳（　　　　　　　　　　　　　　　　　　　　）

2 ________________________________

和訳（　　　　　　　　　　　　　　　　　　　　）

3 ________________________________

和訳（　　　　　　　　　　　　　　　　　　　　）

Unit 4 Scotland

Unit 4 Scotland Chapter 10 Tattoo Festival

After the afternoon session of day one at the university, Ryu and the other teachers got together at 5 p.m. and headed for Edinburgh to watch the Tattoo Festival at the Edinburgh Castle. It took an hour to travel to the historic city. It was a little chilly that day. They walked up the hill paved with stones to a hotel where Dr. Weir's wife was supposed to wait for them. Even at half past 7 o'clock, his wife did not show up, so they became split up for a while. Ryu and his Japanese companions walked along the street to look around for the historic places. His professor was looking for one of the shops where he said they were selling some famous traditional items when the professor had studied abroad there before. Looking back on his rusty memories in those days, he sometimes talked to himself about the location, "Probably I guess the shop was around here; no, it might be over there, but in my memory it can be around here ..."

"The shop might have been closed for good. It was many years ago that you visited Edinburgh the last time, Professor. Your memory has

Tattoo Festival

gradually been deteriorating because of your age ...” Ryu said ironically.

“Mm..., but I think it is around here, judging from the scenery here,” the professor was talking to himself without responding to Ryu’s ironical joke at all. Usually, he talks back to Ryu’s ironic comments or jokes, but in this case the professor probably could not afford to reply to him as usual because he was serious about locating the shop.

Finally, they ended up failing to find the memorable place which the professor often visited during his laborious overseas studies. They could not help giving it up and decided to get a bite of light supper before the festival started. Ryu purchased some bread and juice at a small shop. They went back to the hotel where Dr. Weir had promised to meet his wife.

Though they kept waiting for her in the lobby, she never showed up. As Dr. Weir mentioned, she seemed to have taken the wrong train to go to Edinburgh. Helplessly, they went up the long stone-covered street toward Edinburgh Castle, leaving without his wife. On their way to the castle, there were a lot of young people selling pamphlets about the Tattoo Festival. They were shouting something like ‘Tattoo Pro / Bro ...” hoisting the pamphlet in the air. Ryu could not clearly catch what they were saying. Then the professor said to Ryu, “What are they saying, I wonder.” After a while he said again, “I got it. They are saying, ‘Tattoo Program’.”

Afterwards, what they saw there was a huge temporary stand like the Colosseum of the ancient Roman Empire. On the opposite side of the stadium was the gorgeous castle; on the other three sides of the square was the temporary spectators’ stadium. They climbed up the steep stairs to get to their seats by just following the group in front of them.

The Tattoo Festival stadium was so crowded that even though they sat in their own seats, they felt trapped in them. Ryu had brought bread and juice for a light supper, but he was sitting in such a tight space that he did not feel like eating it or taking it out of his rucksack. At one time he tried to put on his sweat shirt because it was cold, but he had quite some difficulty in putting it on and felt uncomfortable because of the crowded conditions.

At last the Tattoo Festival started. They recognized the starting because the MC gave an announcement about the Tattoo Festival. He tried to, in a sense, stir up the spectators there in order to liven up the festival by saying this:

> "Ladies and gentlemen, welcome to the Tattoo Festival. We appreciate your kindness to come all the way here from various countries. Thank you for coming from far-away countries. ... Welcome to the festival, people from Chili. (Those people waved and cheered.) Thank you for coming to the festival, people from Switzerland. ... (Finally, it is time to listen to the name of the country, Japan.) Welcome to the festival, people coming from Japan." (They shouted, "Hew, hew ..." and cheered waving their hands.)

Tattoo Festival (2)

The audience was so excited, waving and cheering, that they gradually got involved in the cheering atmosphere. It was extremely exciting and thrilling. Quite a few of the army marching bands and dancing people in the parade had come from various countries. Above all, Ryu was very moved by the performance of the Swiss Army band. They had played the drums, both big and small, while marching neatly back and forth, or circling in a chorus. Sometimes they handed their sticks to the next drummer while playing at the same time. Before they knew it, the audience was clapping their hands. Though they were absorbed in the skillful performance, it was getting chilly or even cold enough for Ryu to have to wear his sweat shirt.

Vocabulary Check

英単語に合う意味を右の日本語から選び，(　　　) に記号を記入しなさい。

1 chilly	(　　　)	a.	司会者
2 rusty	(　　　)	b.	高く掲げる
3 deteriorate	(　　　)	c.	豪華な
4 ironical	(　　　)	d.	一時的な，臨時の
5 helplessly	(　　　)	e.	さびついた
6 hoist	(　　　)	f.	活気を与える
7 temporary	(　　　)	g.	皮肉な
8 gorgeous	(　　　)	h.	仕方なく
9 MC	(　　　)	i.	悪化する
10 liven up	(　　　)	j.	肌寒い

Listening Section　英文をよく聞いて，英語で答えよう。

1 ______________________________

2 ______________________________

3 ______________________________

4 ______________________________

Reading Comprehension

本文をよく読んで，次の問いに日本語で答えよう。

1 龍の教授が，かつて知っていた店が見つからなかった時，龍が言った皮肉めいた言葉は何でしたか。

2 エジンバラ城行く途中，たくさんの若者は何をしていましたか。

3 司会者が日本から来た人を紹介した時，日本人は何をしましたか。

4 龍がとても感動したバンドは，どこのバンドで，彼らは何をしましたか。

Speaking Section

本文に合うように空所を埋めよう。但し，下線部には 2 語以上入る。その後，龍（Ryu）になったつもりで，パートナー（A）と対話をしてみよう。

<Part 1>

A: Ryu, I heard you went to Scotland with your friends last year. What did you see there?

Ryu: We went to see the ________________________ at ______________________.

A: Tattoo Festival? What is it? Does it mean participants tattoo the (   )?

Ryu: No, no. That's a different meaning. In this case, this means '(   )'. But before we went there, we had some trouble.

A: What happened, Ryu?

Ryu: We were supposed to ______________________ at a hotel at 7 p.m. But ______________________ did not show up even by half past 7 p.m.

A: How did you deal with it?

Ryu: We just waited for a while. Actually, my (   ) told us he would show us one of the shops and we walked around the city of (   ). But unfortunately he could not find the shop.

A: Why?

Ryu: I think it's because his memory has been gradually (   ).

A: You must be kidding.

<Part 2>

A: Tell me more about the Tattoo Festival at Edinburgh Castle, Ryu.

Ryu: OK. The huge ______________________ was set up at the castle. It was like the Colosseum of the ______________________________.

A: Wow! That sounds gorgeous.

Ryu: Yes, it surely was. The Tattoo Festival was so crowded that we

________________________ in there.

A: Did you sit there eating and drinking?

Ryu: I bought some (　　　　　　) and (　　　　　　) for a light supper, but it was a little hard to eat and drink there.

A: Even so, I think you had a good time watching the festival.

Ryu: Of course. The (　　　　　　) gave an announcement about the festival and it started around 8 o'clock. He had a good technique to ________________________ the spectators.

A: Really? How did he do it?

Ryu: He first called the names of the (　　　　　　　　) which the spectators came from and then aroused them to action by __________________________.

A: I felt like going to see that festival now.

Grammar Section

ここでは強調構文の学習をしよう。**It is (was)～that** の強調構文は，強調したい語句を It is (was)と that の間に入れる。本文中の例文で確認しよう。

It was many years ago **that** you visited Edinburgh the last time.
（あなたが前回エジンバラを訪れたのは，何年も前だったよ。）

that の他にも挿入する語句によって，主語の場合 who，時を示す副詞句の場合 when, 場所を示す語句の場合 where, 目的語の場合 which などが使われる。

It is Maki **who** comes to the office the earliest every morning.
（毎朝最初に出社するは真紀だ。）

It was in 1914 **when** World War I broke out.
（第一次世界大戦が勃発したのは 1914 年だった。）

Arrange Words

（　　　　）内の語を並べ替えて，正しい英文にしよう。

1 (was, World, that, during, it, War, II) his son died.

2 (that, I, it, yesterday, met, was) her at the post office.

3 (made, was, that, the typhoon, us, it) stay at the hotel yesterday.

Writing Section

ここでは次の英語表現を学ぼう。

> **cannot help～ing**，**cannot (help) but** 動詞（原形）の形で「～せざるをえない」「しないではいられない」という意味を表す。例文で確認しよう。
>
> They **could not help** giving it up.（彼らはそれを諦めざるをえなかった。）
>
> They **could not help but** use non-verbal communication.
>
> （彼らは非言語コミュニケーションを使わざるをえなかった。）

それでは，学習した英語表現を使って練習しよう。次の状況で英文を書いてみよう。

1　あなたは，今まで使っていたノートパソコンが壊れてしまいました。そこで新しいノートパソコンを購入せざるを得ません。このことをI cannot help …で始めて，英語で表現してみよう。

2　あなたは，英語力，特にリスニング力の向上を考えています。そこで，毎日ラジオで英会話番組を聞かないではいられないと考えています。このことをI cannot help but …で始めて，英語で表現してみよう。

Dictation Section

英語を聞いて書き取ってみよう。その英文の意味も書こう。

1 ______________________________

和訳（　　　　　　　　　　　　　　　　　　　　　　　）

2 ______________________________

和訳（　　　　　　　　　　　　　　　　　　　　　　　）

3 ______________________________

和訳（　　　　　　　　　　　　　　　　　　　　　　　）

Unit 4 Scotland Chapter 11 Presentation and Dr. Weir's House

That night Ryu had dinner with Dr. Ozasa and the other teachers. Of course, Norika, whose baggage was missing, showed up at the dinner. When he saw her for the first time on the trip, she was not cheerful and tended to look down to the ground; she was very gloomy. He knew how she was feeling about the missing luggage now, since he had the same bitter experience in Australia as follows:

> At that time his baggage was missing and the staff member at the airport told him then that his suitcase might have gone to another airport. He continued to say, "Never mind. You can get it soon. Please wait for a while." On that day he had no underwear to change into after taking a bath; he looked for men's underpants at a small drugstore, but he could not find them. Ryu was compelled to buy women's underwear because he was used to sleeping in clean underpants at night, but he could only find women's.

Mr. Seishin at George Square

Ryu told the others about his experience with his underwear later that night. It may have relieved her feelings a little to hear the story. Norika gave a little smile to him at that time, but she soon looked gloomy. Since then, in his mind, Ryu called her Ms. Gloomy. Later he told her out about his joke when she was beginning to get more cheerful.

In the morning Ryu wandered around George Square to purchase some gifts at the Information Center. Then it happened that he saw Mr. Seishin reading his academic paper in the square. He was practicing very seriously with the manuscript in his left hand and using gestures with his right hand up and down. Ryu tried to approach him to say hello to him, but instantly Ryu gave it up. Even though there was a very beautiful Scottish lady close to Mr. Seishin, he continued to ignore her and kept practicing for the paper. (In reality, he might have been very nervous about reading his paper, but nobody could read his mind. That was just like Mr. Seishin.) It is worthwhile to really respect him for his enthusiasm for the research presentation. There he appeared to be an authority on the English Language Field; the serious aura he produced did not allow Ryu to get close to him. So Ryu just took a photo as proof that the professor was a very studious and meticulous speaker, sparing no pains in preparing for the presentation. He respected Mr. Seishin for his strenuous efforts and positive attitude toward the conference.

Ryu had butterflies in his stomach that day. It is tough to make a presentation in English even for a person who has got used to it. He thought he would have to be like his professor, who often said he felt excited and had goose bumps in the international conference. He was sure that he needed to undergo more discipline and training to become a presenter of that kind, one who can keep his amiable composure like his professor's. Before Ryu's speech, his friend, Mr. Seishin from Japan pulled off a good presentation at the workshop in the afternoon. The next speaker, Ryu also did well with his presentation at the workshop in spite of his great anxiety. He asked his colleagues to take pictures during his presentation. His professor said to Ryu later, "Your appearance at the lectern looked like you were full of confidence, and you did a much better job than when you presented in Beijing." Ryu was very happy to hear his professor's compliments and at the same time he was determined to study more in order to give a better presentation at the next conference.

After the workshop, they took a train bound for Ayr, where Dr. Weir lives. It took approximately fifty minutes to reach the town from Glasgow. It was a nice and calm town, and Ryu took in the fresh air after getting off the train. But it was a little dark in the evening and they saw some streetlights were on. They decided to use taxis to get to his house.

When Ryu and the others reached his house, they saw the Scottish professor's wife waiting for them, standing at the gate. They took off their shoes at the entrance in the Japanese way and shook hands with her, saying, "Nice to meet you." Ryu was looking around the house and the well-kept garden, talking to others. After a while Dr. Weir ushered them to the second floor of the house, where many traditional Japanese things such as ukiyo-e-style paintings and cups were exhibited. This proved how much interest he took in Japan. Drinking wine or beer, he also showed the Japanese guests some pictures in which his family was feeding wild birds such as a crow in the garden at the back of the house. It looked as if he was very proud of it.

Dinner was ready; they were seated at the table according to Dr. Weir's instructions. Every time they talked, the Scottish professor played an active and key role in the conversation. Ryu believed the professor had great mental agility, since he could pick up the topic people were talking about and provided a witty remark, which made others all laugh. But sometimes Ryu couldn't follow his good witticisms. He remembered one of his jokes (wits) at the table. They were talking about one of the foods served there, haggis.

Then his professor said, "This haggis is less tasty. Whisky should be put into the haggis." Dr. Weir immediately responded to him, saying, "It (lamb) doesn't drink." If Ryu had time, he could make a list of Dr. Weir's remarks.

They served a variety of foods: haggis, chicken, boiled potatoes and carrots, and drinks like red wine, beer and whisky. For dessert they served ice cream to Ryu and the other guests.

Ryu left his house for Glasgow at 10:40 at night. He thought everybody had to appreciate the Scottish family's kindness and hospitality to treat them so well.

Vocabulary Check

英単語に合う意味を右の日本語から選び，(　　)に記号を記入しなさい。

1 undergo	(　　)	a.	うろうろする
2 discipline	(　　)	b.	同僚，仲間
3 composure	(　　)	c.	たゆまぬ
4 colleague	(　　)	d.	細心の注意を払って
5 compliment	(　　)	e.	案内する
6 wander	(　　)	f.	機敏さ
7 meticulous	(　　)	g.	受ける
8 strenuous	(　　)	h.	褒め言葉
9 usher	(　　)	i.	鍛錬，修養
10 agility	(　　)	j.	冷静さ，落ち着き

Listening Section　英文をよく聞いて，英語で答えよう。

1 ______________________________

2 ______________________________

3 ______________________________

4 ______________________________

Reading Comprehension

本文をよく読んで，次の問いに日本語で答えよう。

1　龍が友人の Mr. Seishin の写真を密かに撮った理由は何ですか。

2　龍が教授のようになる必要があると考えていますが，その教授はよく何と言っていましたか。

3　龍は，発表後彼の教授に何と言われましたか。

4　ウィア先生が機知の利いた言葉を発する具体的な場面の会話はどんなものでしたか。

Speaking Section

本文に合うように空所を埋めよう。但し，下線部には 2 語以上入る。その後，龍（Ryu）になったつもりで，パートナー（A）と対話をしてみよう。

<Part 1>

A: I heard you participated in the international conference and read your paper.

Ryu: Yes.

A: Did you feel ( ) about reading it?

Ryu: Honestly speaking, I had ____________ stomach that day. Before my presentation, my friend, Mr. Seishin ( ) off a good presentation.

A: Oh, if so, you must have been more nervous about it.

Ryu: In some ways, that's true. Actually, that morning I happened to see Mr. Seishin practicing so seriously ____________ at the George Square.

A: Did you talk to him at that time?

Ryu: No. I could not ( ) him because of his enthusiasm.

A: I understand your feelings.

Ryu: Interestingly enough, he did not notice me at all even on the same square, or he did not see a beautiful ( ) lady standing close to him.

A: Wow! That's unbelievable!

Ryu: So, I took a photo of them from the appropriate angle as a ( ) of his forward-looking attitude toward the presentation.

A: That's an idea! Did you show him the photo later?

Ryu: Yes, of course. When he saw the picture, he kept laughing for a while with me.

<Part 2>

A: Where did you go after the workshop?

Ryu: We visited (   ), who is a close friend of my professor.

A: How long did it take to get to his town from Glasgow?

Ryu: It took about ______________________ to reach the town. To our surprise, when we reached his house, we had to ______________________________ at the entrance like in Japan.

A: Really? How (   ) they have that kind of custom?

Ryu: I'm not sure, but I think he will take ________________________ in Japan.

A: Does he collect ___________________________ things?

Ryu: Yes. We saw so many Japan-related things were exhibited such as ukiyo-e-style (   ) and (   ).

A: That makes sense.

Grammar Section

ここでは時制の一致の学習をしよう。「時制の一致」は，原則，主節の時制が過去の場合，従属節もそれに合わせて変化していくことである。例えば，本文中には次のような英文がある。

He thought he would have to be like his professor.

（彼は彼の教授のようにならなければならないと思った。）

主節が現在形の場合は，その時点で未来のことを語っているので will を使用することになる。つまり，次のような英文になる。

He thinks he will have to be like his professor.

時制の一致をしない場合は，次のような場合がある。

(1)現在の事実や一般的な真理　The students knew that the earth goes around the sun.

(2)現在の習慣　He said that he takes a walk every morning.

(3)過去の事実　The teacher told us that World War II ended in 1945.

Arrange Words

（　　　　）内の語を並べ替えて，正しい英文にしよう。

1 The (water, that, learned, boils, pupils) at 100℃.

2 (light, that, daughter, said, has, Tom, his) blue eyes.

3 My (see, it, that, to, was, told, friend, me, exciting) the movie.

Writing Section

ここでは次の英語表現を学ぼう。

have (got) butterflies in one's stomach（ドキドキしている，ハラハラしている）；**have a frog in one's throat**（声がしわがれている）；**have a maggot in one's head**（気まぐれな考えを抱く）などがある。本文中の例文で確認してみよう。

Ryu had butterflies in his stomach today.（龍はその日ドキドキしていた。）

それでは，学習した英語表現を使って練習しよう。次の状況で英文を書いてみよう。

1　あなたは，友人の結婚披露宴でいよいよ挨拶する番が近づいています。今ドキドキして逃げ出したい気分になっています。このことをI have ...で始めて，英語で表現してみよう。

2　あなたは，今日はのどの調子があまり良くないようです。何度咳払いしても，いまだにしわがれ声のままです。このことをEven though I clear...で始めて，英語で表現してみよう。

Dictation Section

英語を聞いて書き取ってみよう。その英文の意味も書こう。

1 ____

和訳（　　　　　　　　　　　　　　　　　　　　）

2 ____

和訳（　　　　　　　　　　　　　　　　　　　　）

3 ____

和訳（　　　　　　　　　　　　　　　　　　　　）

Unit 4 Scotland　Chapter 12 One-day Trip

Ryu took a one-day trip to Dublin with his friends. They waited at the bus stop, close to George Square. They had promised to meet Mr. and Mrs. Weir at Glasgow Airport. While waiting to see them, Ryu went to the restroom and then bought a local newspaper and a bottle of water. But that was a mistake, because passengers were not permitted to bring liquids on the airplane. Before Ryu went through inspection at the check-in counter, he had to throw it away in a trash can.

At the security check, passengers were requested to spread their arms horizontally and they were checked all over by being touched on their shirt, trousers and everywhere by the people in charge. Also, they had to take off their shoes, jackets and even take out their wallets. One of the female passengers standing in front of Ryu was checked all over by a female staff member at the airport. When she was checked, the airport staff raised up this chubby passenger's bloated shirt over her belly. Ryu guessed she

Scottish Man Playing the Bagpipe

might have thought the passenger had something around her belly. The woman seemed to be feeling something strange about the staff member groping for something around the potbelly. In reality she was just fat; therefore, she began to laugh when she was being checked. It sounded funny to Ryu as well, and he chuckled a little at her.

During the flight, Ryu read an article in the newspaper about a heavy influx of people into the United Kingdom. He read this interesting article that compared the situation in the UK with that of Japan. It took less than two hours to fly to the destination, Dublin.

Ryu and the others first took a bus and went to the city center. Then, they walked around the town. However, it was so crowded there that it was not easy to move forward together in a group, walking abreast. The tourists as well as local people were passing by each other everywhere in town. When people were coming toward them on the street, Ryu had to think how he should try to avoid the people.

They had lunch at the Madison pub, which the famous novelist, James Joyce frequently visited in his life. The proof of the fact is that quite a few black and white photos of the writer were attached to the pub walls and in the toilets. Ryu ordered chicken and bacon and the others ate whatever they wanted to. Dr. Weir treated them to a pint of Guinness beer and they had a good time talking and eating together there. Around 2 p.m., they left the pub and walked along the main busy street. The center of the town has a tall tower or pole called Stiletto Tower, which Ryu had heard was established in 2000.

They decided to assemble at a meeting spot at around 4:00 p.m. and then split up to go their own way. Ryu walked with Mr. Seishin along the street which was extremely crowded with tourists. They talked a lot about their work and what happened at their universities while working there. He treated Ryu to an orange juice at a pub before they went to the designated meeting place. It seemed to him that talking to Mr. Seishin at such a comfortable place gave Ryu great comfort and energy. Ryu thought Mr. Seishin would be very popular among the students at his university, judging from his joyous temperament and positive attitude toward teaching and working. Then Ryu bought magnets with Irish scenery and an Ireland-shaped plate with a frame at the Information Center.

When they went back to the airport, Ryu sat next to the graduate student, Graham, in the front seat on a bus. Then they talked a lot about topics like driving and history and culture in Scotland and Ireland. Regarding driving, Graham did not have a driver's license. The student said, "I don't need it. I didn't need it when I was a college student." That may be true in a sense, but Ryu thought sooner or later he would probably need a driver's license when trying to land a job. Of course, some or a few people still don't need it, in which case they can use public transportation like a bus or a train.

The bus driver drove very fast on the motorway and on the regular roads as well. The speed limit was 70 miles per hour, which meant 112 km/h. Ryu figured that was why they were driving so fast. He talked to the graduate student about his serious car accidents when he was commuting to his former workplace in Japan.

> One day when Ryu was driving back home, he was so exhausted from hard work that he gradually felt he was getting sleepy. He was at the point of dozing off. Thirty minutes after he left the school, he began to feel it might be better to pull over and rest for a while. But he continued to drive, pinching his cheeks to stay awake. That was the wrong choice. After a while he began to nod off while driving, so he

did not notice the car in front of him was stopping. He struck the car from the back, then that car hit another one in front of it, and that car hit the next car in front of it. Due to his careless driving, three car drivers were involved in the troublesome accident, or the four-car collision. Ryu shouted in his mind, "Oh, my gosh!" Fortunately, no one was injured in the accident. Of course, one woman felt a pain in her neck later and went to the hospital.

Vocabulary Check

英単語に合う意味を右の日本語から選び，(　　　)に記号を記入しなさい。

1 doze	(　　　　)	a. 極端に
2 horizontally	(　　　　)	b. 手探りする
3 chubby	(　　　　)	c. 居眠りをする
4 bloated	(　　　　)	d. 気質，性分
5 belly	(　　　　)	e. 流入
6 grope	(　　　　)	f. 集合する
7 influx	(　　　　)	g 水平に
8 assemble	(　　　　)	h. お腹
9 extremely	(　　　　)	i. 小太りの
10 temperament	(　　　　)	j. 膨らんだ

Listening Section　英文をよく聞いて，英語で答えよう。

1 ______________________________

2 ______________________________

3 ______________________________

4 ______________________________

Reading Comprehension

本文をよく読んで，次の問いに日本語で答えよう。

1　空港の安全検査で，乗客は何をすることを要求されましたか。

2　龍は，午後4時の集合まで誰とどのような行動をしましたか。

3　龍は，どこでどんな土産を買いましたか。

4　バスのスピードが速かった理由は何ですか。

Speaking Section

本文に合うように空所を埋めよう。但し，下線部には 2 語以上入る。その後，龍（Ryu）になったつもりで，パートナー（A）と対話をしてみよう。

<Part 1>

A: Did you go to Dublin, Ryu?

Ryu: Yes. It was a ________________ to Dublin because of our tight schedule.

A: How did you get to the airport?

Ryu: We got on a bus at the nearest bus stop at __________________. When I arrived at Glasgow Airport, I bought a newspaper and a ____________________. That was a mistake.

A: Why do you say such a thing?

Ryu: Actually, we could not bring (   ) on the airplane.

A: That's too bad.

Ryu: I had a funny story about one female passenger.

A: Please tell me about it in detail.

Ryu: OK. This is what happened at the ______________. She was a (   ) person and the staffer at the airport thought she had something around her (   ).

A: And then?

Ryu: The person began ____________ something around it. The woman felt something strange about the staff's groping and began to laugh. I also chuckled a little then.

A: But I think the staffer took his job seriously.

Ryu: You're telling me.

<Part 2>

A: Where did you go in Dublin?

Ryu: First, we visited the __________________ and then we walked around the town.

A: How was it?

Ryu: I did not feel ( ) walking around there.

A: How come you felt uncomfortable?

Ryu: It was ________________ that we couldn't go forward in a group easily. We had to think how we should try to ___________________ coming toward us.

A: I don't like the situation, either.

Ryu: Anyway, we had lunch at the pub called ( ). It's a very well-known pub, because the ______________________ James Joyce often visited there.

A: I have never read his novels. Do you know his writings, Ryu?

Ryu: Well ... Um ... I know one of them. That is Ulyses, but I have never read it.

A: Anyway, what did you order at the pub?

Ryu: I ordered ( ) and bacon. Dr. Weir treated us to a pint of _____________________.

Grammar Section

ここでは動詞の学習をしよう。動詞には自動詞と他動詞がある。自動詞は「S＋V」の文型で使用し，他動詞は目的語をとる動詞である。

They **moved** to the bus stop.（自動詞）

They **reached** Glasgow Airport.（他動詞）

しかし，動詞を使えるようにするためには，個々の動詞の用法を学習する必要がある。例えば，他動詞の後に「to 不定詞」「that 節」「目的語＋to 不定詞」「疑問詞節」が続くもの等々，多岐にわたる。本文中の例文で確認してみよう。

Ryu figured that was why they were driving so fast.
（龍は，それが彼らがあんなに速く運転している理由だと思った。）

They decided to assemble at a meeting spot around 4 p.m.
（彼らは，午後 4 時頃集合場所に集まることに決めた。）

Arrange Words

(　　　　)内の語を並べ替えて，正しい英文にしよう。

1 I (the, that, health, important, is, think, good, most) thing in our life.

2 You (married, tell, to, to, her, get, should) her boyfriend as soon as possible.

3 The (live, us, how, taught, to, teacher) a better future life.

Writing Section

ここでは次の英語表現を学ぼう。

so ～that ... （たいへん～なので...）の構文は，so の後に形容詞か副詞がくる。本文中の例文で確認してみよう。

It was so crowded there **that** it was not easy to move forward.
（そこはとても混雑していたので，前に進むことが容易ではなかった。）

同じ意味の表現に **such ～that ...** がある。この構文は，「such a 形容詞＋名詞」の形で使用されることが多い。

それでは，学習した英語表現を使って練習しよう。次の状況で英文を書いてみよう。

1　あなたの友人のキム君（Kim）は，とても走るのが速く，運動会のレースで負けたことはありません。このことを Kim is such ...で始めて，英語で表現してみよう。

2　その山はとても険しい山だから，誰も登りたがりません。このことを The mountain is so ...で始めて，英語で表現してみよう。

Dictation Section

英語を聞いて書き取ってみよう。その英文の意味も書こう。

1 ____________________

和訳（　　　　　　　　　　　　　　　　　　）

2 ____________________

和訳（　　　　　　　　　　　　　　　　　　）

3 ____________________

和訳（　　　　　　　　　　　　　　　　　　）

Unit 5 Vietnam

Unit 5 Vietnam Chapter 13 Visit to Village

Ryu had a great chance to visit a local village on the outskirts of Hanoi by bus. The roads in the rural areas were not well-organized and he was annoyed by the bumpy roads. Ryu sometimes felt uncomfortable as if his intestines would bounce out of his mouth because of the rough roads. It took him more than two hours to get to the destination. The moment he arrived at the village, he was warmly welcomed by the local people, especially the innocent children. Or rather, they seemed to be curious about Ryu, who was a stranger to them. Unfortunately, they could not easily communicate with each other because he could not speak Vietnamese, and the children could not speak English. That was why they could not help but use non-verbal communication, such as eye contact and a lot of gestures. That was the only means by which they had to understand each other at that time.

One of the families invited Ryu into their home. When he entered the wooden house, they served him a cold drink and some local dishes.

It seemed that this was the traditional or conventional way to treat guests.

Vietnamese Girl Carrying Vegetables

First, they gave a toast to his health and success, and then meat was served to him for lunch. He heard that meat is rare and valuable for local people in Vietnam since they eat it only once a week. A bowl of meat was served in front of him. He first put rice paper (*Banh la*) on a leaf and then placed meat and a tiny spicy leaf on it. The spicy flavor went well with the meat and it was delicious.

He saw a lot of chickens freely walking around the house, with no fence. He wondered if the villagers could recognize their own poultry when they walked about freely in the village. In all likelihood, the villagers could distinguish them by their feathers or features.

After lunch he climbed a steep mountain behind their house with the local children in hot weather. They guided him to the mountain nearby, and he tried to just follow the children, producing a lot of sweat. It took about 15 minutes to get to the summit of the mountain. Ryu had a magnificent view of the village and mountains far away from him, which almost completely made him forget his tiredness and his effort to climb up.

After descending, the innocent children poured water from the well over themselves or drank it. He was shocked at the water that one of the girls drew from the well. Though the color of the water was creamy like milk, she started to gulp it down without hesitation. He thought that if he drank the water, he would get diarrhea immediately. Probably, they already have resistance against the bacteria and viruses found in that dirty water.

After he finished visiting the village, Ryu decided to go to Kanh Street in Hanoi. On his way to the street he happened to see lean boys with a wooden box under their arms. From a little distance he was wondering what they were doing carrying wooden boxes. Therefore, Ryu asked them what the boxes were for, pointing at them. The moment they opened the box, he noticed they polished shoes. When Ryu was walking away, they followed him. Helplessly, he asked one of them, “How much?” One of the boys gave him a quick reply like this, “Two dollar(s).” He thought it was a little expensive, so Ryu said, "Dah quwa (too expensive)." The other boy responded to him, "No, no. cheap, cheap." He continued to say, "Dah quwa." Then the boy thought over for a while and asked him, "How much?" Ryu responded to him, "One dollar." The boy was unwilling to say, "OK." Finally, he had two boys polish his leather shoes paying one dollar each.

After that Ryu walked away from them, but from somewhere another teenage boy approached him to try to polish his shoes. He did not have to have them polished, so he refused the boy's offer. Then Ryu wanted to take photos of being together as a good memory in Hanoi. He happened to see the Vietnamese boys who had polished his shoes coming to him again. He thought he was lucky and waved to them, saying, "Come here. Let's take a picture together." Ryu saw Vietnamese women dealing in business across the road and they seemed to be staring at Ryu, wondering what he was doing with the boys. While he took out his camera and was checking the distance between the camera and the teenagers, one of the women already came over to Ryu. He noticed that she was standing beside him and wondered how she crossed the busy street. She meant she would take photos of Ryu and the boys, using gestures. Ryu played upon her kindness and asked her to take photos using gestures and saying, "Press this button, please."

It took her time to take photos of them, partly because maybe they were not in the frame of the camera. Therefore, she began to go back little by little and finally she almost reached around the middle of the busy road. Ryu was so concerned about her that he could not focus on the lens of the camera. As she went back, his heart was beating harder. He almost shouted to her, "You went back a little too far." Lots of cars and motorcycles were running on the wide street. He was very impressed to see the Vietnamese thoughtfulness and kindness to one foreign tourist like him. She came all the way from the other side of the traffic-choked street to just take photos of them. If she was a Japanese person, would she have done the same thing as the Vietnamese woman did under the circumstances like that? He thought that Vietnamese people probably had more spiritual richness than Japanese people even though they were economically poor.

Vocabulary Check

英単語に合う意味を右の日本語から選び，（　　）に記号を記入しなさい。

1 bumpy	（　　　）	a. いやいやながらの
2 conventional	（　　　）	b. 思いやり
3 distinguish	（　　　）	c. 因習的な
4 innocent	（　　　）	d. 状況
5 thoughtfulness	（　　　）	e. でこぼこの
6 circumstances	（　　　）	f. 皮
7 unwilling	（　　　）	g. 無邪気な
8 leather	（　　　）	h. 家禽
9 poultry	（　　　）	i. 区別する
10 steep	（　　　）	j. 険しい

Listening Section　英文をよく聞いて，英語で答えよう。

1 ______________________________

2 ______________________________

3 ______________________________

4 ______________________________

Reading Comprehension

本文をよく読んで，次の問いに日本語で答えよう。

1　ベトナムの村の道路をバスで走っている時，龍はどのような気分でしたか。

2　龍は，どのようにして村の人々とコミュニケーションをとりましたか。

3　ベトナムの少年が箱を開けたとき，龍はその中に何を見たとあなたは思いますか。

4　龍は，日本人と比べて，ベトナム人に対する印象についてどう述べていますか。

Speaking Section

本文に合うように空所を埋めよう。但し，下線部には 2 語以上入る。その後，龍（Ryu）になったつもりで，パートナー（A）と対話をしてみよう。

<Part 1>

A: Where did you go last summer?

Ryu: I went to (   ).

A: Wow! It must have been exciting.

Ryu: Oh, yes. I met ____________________ in a village.

A: Did you talk to them?

Ryu: Umm... No. They did not speak (   ). So we used ____________________.

A: What is ____________________?

Ryu: It means eye contact and (   ).

A: Oh, I see. Ryu, what did you see in the village?

Ryu: I saw domestic poultry.

A: What kind of domestic poultry did they keep?

Ryu: They kept (   ). The poultry were (   ) around the house freely with no (   ).

A: Wow! That's exciting! I want to see it. What else did you do in the village?

Ryu: I climbed a ____________________ with local (   ).

A: That sounds nice. How long did it take to get to the top?

Ryu: I think it took about (   ) minutes. We had a (   ) view of the village and mountains.

A: If you have photos you took there, please show me some.

Ryu: OK. Next time I will show you some beautiful pictures.

A: Thanks.

<Part 2>

A: Ryu, did you walk around Hanoi?

Ryu: Yes. I walked a little on Kanh Street in the city. Then I met some ( ) boys with a ( ) box under their ( ).

A: Did you talk to them on the street?

Ryu: Mm..., it was a little hard to talk to each other. But they followed me there.

A: What were they doing on the street?

Ryu: They were ( ) shoes to ______________________.

A: Uh, huh. Did you have your shoes ( )?

Ryu: Finally, yes. That was good. I was very satisfied with the clean shoes.

A: Did the boys ( ) happy to earn money?

Ryu: That's right. I think they were also satisfied with the job.

Grammar Section

仮定法過去と仮定法過去完了について学習しよう。基本的なパターンは次のとおりである。

仮定法過去「**if** 主語+過去形，主語+**would** 動詞」（**would** は **could, might** も可能）

のパターンで使用し，現在の事実と反対のことや不可能に近いことを仮定するときに使用する。

仮定法過去完了「**if** 主語+**had** 過去分詞，主語+**would have** 過去分詞」（**would** は **could, might** も可能）のパターンで使用し，過去の事実と反対のことを仮定するときに使用する。

仮定法過去「If he drank the water, he would get diarrhea immediately.」

（もし彼がその水を飲めば，すぐに下痢になるだろうに。）

「実際には飲んでいないので、下痢にはなっていない」ことを暗示している。

仮定法過去完了「If he had not met the kind person, he would not have succeeded in business.」（もし彼がその親切な人に会っていなかったら，商売

で成功していなかったであろう。)

「実際には彼がその親切な人に会ったので、商売で成功を収めた」ことを暗示している。このように，過去の出来事に反することを仮定するときに「仮定法過去完了」を使用する。

他にも「**If it were not for ～**」(～がなければ)，「**if it had not been for ～**」(～がなかったら) のような英文パターンがある。

また，**As if** 主語+過去形 (まるで～であるかのように)；**As if** 主語+過去完了形 (まるで～であったかのように) のパターンも覚えておこう。

She talks **as if** she **knew** everything about that country.

(彼女は，その国について何でも知っているかのように話す。)

Arrange Words

(　　　　) 内の語を並べ替えて、正しい英文にしよう。

1 If you (the store, would, spent, gone, not, not, had, you, have, to) so much money.

2 He (studied, talks, before, had, if, abroad, as, he).

3 If (not, would, for, food, were, die, it, all, us, of) soon.

Writing Section

ここでは次の英語表現を学ぼう。

「**The moment S'+V', S+V** 」のパターンで「～したとたん・・・」「～するとすぐに・・・」の意味を表す。接続詞的な役割を果たすので，この語句の後には「主語＋動詞」が続く。他にも **the instant～, as soon as～, the minute～**などの表現もある。例文を見てみよう。

The moment he arrived at the village, he was warmly welcomed by the local people.

（その村に着いたとたん，彼は地元の人々に温かく歓迎された。）

また，**hardly[scarcely]～when[before]...**や **no sooner～than...**で，同様な意味を表す。次の例文のように，過去完了形を使用することが多いので注意しよう。

He had **hardly** got to the station **when** the train started.

（彼が駅に着くとすぐに，その電車は出発した。）

それでは，学習した英語表現を使って練習しよう。次の状況で英文を書いてみよう。

1　あなたは京都を旅行しています。ある神社を訪れました。そこに着いたとたん，その神社の荘厳さに圧倒されました。このことを The moment ...で始めて，英語で表現してみよう。

2　あなたの友人が，夕食会に誘ってくれました。課題レポート済んだらすぐに夕食会に行くつもりです。このことを As soon as...で始めて，英語で表現してみよう。

Dictation Section

英語を聞いて書き取ってみよう。その英文の意味も書こう。

1 ______________________________

和訳（　　　　　　　　　　　　　　　　　）

2 ______________________________

和訳（　　　　　　　　　　　　　　　　　）

3 ______________________________

和訳（　　　　　　　　　　　　　　　　　）

Unit 5 Vietnam Chapter 14 Workshop and Eateries in Hue

Ryu visited one of the popular cities, Hue to participate in the teaching workshop as well as do some sightseeing. They did a lot of pair work at the participatory workshop, but he did not have a partner in the activities. One of the female teachers talked to him from nearby to urge him to positively join the activities. After 30 minutes or so, she asked a question of him in Vietnamese for no reason. Ryu did not completely understand her and he could not say a word. Probably he looked a little bit strange to her, so she seemed to have noticed he was not Vietnamese. Then she said, “Sorry, I thought you were Vietnamese. You look like a Vietnamese person.” In response, he said with a little surprise, “Really?” “Yes,” she said with a smile. Ryu had mixed feelings at that time.

After the workshop, Ryu and his friend, Mike, first wanted to move back to their hotels. Therefore, Mike asked a female staffer to call for a taxi

Restaurant Hot Tuna

by cell phone. She said, “Please wait for ten minutes.” While they were waiting for their taxi, one taxi after another came to the front of the main building, where they picked up passengers. The university premises were a long way from the downtown and were surrounded by beautiful nature. From the different perspective, it could be said they did not have any buildings around the campus, except for small houses for local people. All they had to do was call a taxi to go back to each hotel.

Ryu and his friend talked about a specific plan after the workshop. They thought they should go back to the hotels to leave their bags with a little heavy computer in their rooms. Then they tried to get into a taxi which one of the university staff members called for them at the gate of the university, which was 300 meters away from the main building. The female staffer told them to go there since their taxi was waiting for them. Therefore, they walked along on the seemingly rough university path made out of red soil. While moving toward the gate, Ryu saw a green taxi coming there. He shouted, “That's it! Our taxi! Green one.”

They rushed to the cab stopping at the university gate and quickly tried to get into the taxi, but the cabdriver refused their ride. Using his body language, he showed it was not their taxi, which meant the taxi was reserved for another customer. Mike ignored the driver's behavior and swiftly got in. He also requested Ryu to get into the taxi. His friend said to the driver in a strong tone, “OK. Go! Go!” However, the driver, opening the doors ajar, demanded that they should get out of it. Ryu was hesitating to get out of it since his friend told strongly him to stay in and said, “Let's go! Go!” His remarks meant that the driver should get the car moving, and at the same time they put Ryu under more pressure, in a sense.

Then, the driver drove to the entrance of the university building with them on and he asked the female student standing there in Vietnamese whether they would be allowed to get into the taxi. The Vietnamese student explained to other passengers about the confusing situation and they agreed with her. All got in and went toward each passenger's hotel. His friend told everybody repeatedly, "OK. OK. We pay the taxi charge. Never mind. We are the last passengers to get out of the taxi. Ha, ha ha ..."

After other passengers got off, Ryu and Mike finally reached Holiday Hotel, where his friend was staying. A female staffer at the reception desk looked at Ryu and at once said, "Are you Vietnamese? You look like our people." "Really?" he responded to her. He added, "At the workshop I was told the same thing by a female participant."

Eventually, sadly or amazingly, Ryu was mistaken for a Vietnamese person four times during his stay in Hue. He thought that perhaps it might be commonplace to see Vietnamese people who resembled him with a thin face. He was wondering if he should be happy or sad about this. Then Ryu met other tourists from Japan at the entrance and moved out of the hotel.

While they were wandering about to find a nice and reasonable place to drink beer and eat traditional Vietnamese cuisine, two girls who looked like local primary school students, approached them and begged them to buy some traditional Vietnamese pictures using body language. But Ryu ignored the girls and tried to pass along. Just then one of his friends started to open the slides in the ice cream freezer outside the restaurant and he was kind enough to treat the girls to ice cream. He bought ice cream for Ryu, as well. In retrospect he regretted not having bought one of the pictures the girls asked him to buy. This should have been a good memory in Vietnam, as well.

After a while, they were so starved that they tried to enter a restaurant to drink local beer and eat some local Vietnamese dishes. While walking around the local city, they were looking at different types of shops, such as tailor shops and souvenir shops. They happened to stop at the intersection in the busy town where motorcycles were running along the old street, honking their horns. The frequent noises from them gave a great nuisance to him.

Finally, the restaurant called Hot Tuna caught their eyes and they decided to have some dinner after checking out the menu on the podium outside the restaurant. That was located at the corner of the streets and it looked as if it attracted foreign tourists easily. They cheered drinking Hue or Festival beer. Then they had pumpkin soup and steamed thin rice with meat or shrimp. He happened to see a small gecko on the floor and took a photo of the reptile quickly. He found some interesting and artistic works like well-designed paper butterflies and fish around the restaurant and took photos of them.

Hue Beer

Vocabulary Check

英単語に合う意味を右の日本語から選び，(　　)に記号を記入しなさい。

1 premises	(　　　　)	a. 交差点
2 perspective	(　　　　)	b. 爬虫類
3 cabdriver	(　　　　)	c. エビ
4 swiftly	(　　　　)	d. 台
5 ajar	(　　　　)	e. 視点
6 commonplace	(　　　　)	f. 普通の，よく見られる
7 intersection	(　　　　)	g. タクシーの運転手
8 podium	(　　　　)	h. 半開きで
9 shrimp	(　　　　)	i. 敷地
10 reptile	(　　　　)	j. 素早く

Listening Section　英文をよく聞いて，英語で答えよう。

1 ____________________

2 ____________________

3 ____________________

4 ____________________

Reading Comprehension

本文をよく読んで，次の問いに日本語で答えよう。

1　大学のキャンパスはどんな所にありましたか。

2　何故，ワークショップ後，龍たちはホテルに戻ったのですか。

3　2人の小学生らしき女の子は，龍に何を要求してきましたか。

4　龍は，Hot Tuna で飲食以外に何をしましたか。

Speaking Section

本文に合うように空所を埋めよう。但し，下線部には 2 語以上入る。その後，龍（Ryu）になったつもりで，パートナー（A）と対話をしてみよう。

<Part 1>

A: Where did you go this time, Ryu?

Ryu: I went to one of the local cities, (　　　　) in Vietnam.

A: Would you say again?

Ryu: (　　　　). If you like traveling in South East Asia, I think you know the city.

A: I see. Well, what did you do there?

Ryu: I ____________________ the workshop at the local university.

A: Workshop? You are very (　　　　) about teaching English, aren't you?

Ryu: It can't be helped. I am a teacher.

A: Anyhow, after the workshop, what else did you do there?

Ryu: I walked around the local city and had a ________________ talking and eating at restaurants. But before that, we had some trouble at the university.

A: Please tell me about what happened.

Ryu: Let's see... My friend and I asked a ______________________ to call for a taxi. Then we found a ____________________ at the university gate.

A: And then?

Ryu: Then the cabdriver did not accept our (　　　　). But finally, we were accepted.

<Part 2>

A: Did you go to a restaurant, Ryu?

Ryu: Yes. We went to the restaurant, _________________. At that time we were very (　　　　) and we happened to check out the menu outside. We dropped in and drank beer and ate traditional ( ) cuisine.

A: Did it taste good?

Ryu: Of course. It was scramputous.

A: What kind of food did you eat?

Ryu: We had ( ) soup and ______________________ with meat or shrimp.

A: My mouth is ( ).

Ryu: Also, intrestingly enough, I happened to see a ( ) in the restaurant.

A: What is it?

Ryu: It's a kind of ( ). I took several photos of it. Would you like to see them?

A: Yes, of course.

Grammar Section

ここでは不定詞の用法（to+動詞の原形）の学習をしよう。不定詞には大きく分けて３つの用法がある。名詞的用法・形容詞的用法・副詞的用法である。その使い方を確認しよう。

名詞的用法はその名のとおり，名詞的な使い方をする。つまり，主語や目的語・補語の役割をして「～すること」という意味を表す。

Ryu was hesitating to get out of it.（龍はそこから出るのをためらっていた。）

この英文では，「to get」が目的語になっている。

次に，形容詞的用法について説明する。この形容詞的用法は，前の名詞を修飾し，「～する（ための）」「～すべき」などの意味になる。

I wanted something to drink.（私は何か飲み物がほしかった。）

最後に，副詞的用法である。これは，前の動詞や形容詞などを修飾する形をとる。英文によって意味のとり方は異なる。英文で確認をしよう。

Ryu visited Hue to participate in the teaching workshop.

（龍は教育ワークショップに参加するためにフエに行った。）

He was amazed to see her standing beside him.

（彼は自分の背後に彼女が立っているのを見て驚いた。）

Arrange Words

（　　　）内の語を並べ替えて，正しい英文にしよう。

1 We were very (arrived, know, at, to, the airport, that, happy, Tsutomu) in one piece.

2 It is very (time, to, particular, study, a, important, at, every) day.

3 Teenagers (read, provided, books, to, with, be, good, should) while they are young.

Writing Section

ここでは次の英語表現を学ぼう。

「人に～するように頼む」の意味をあらわす表現として，「**ask** 人 **to do**」「**request** 人 **to do**」「**beg** 人 **to do**」などがある。request は ask より堅い語で，beg はへりくだった意味合いがあり，よく「懇願する」と訳される。本文中の例文で確認してみよう。

He also **requsted** Ryu **to** get into the taxi.

（彼は，また龍にタクシーに乗るように要求した。）

Two girls **begged** them **to** buy some traditional Vietnamese pictures.

（二人の少女は，彼らに伝統的なベトナムの絵を買うように懇願した。）

それでは，学習した英語表現を使って練習しよう。次の状況で英文を書いてみよう。

1 あなたの友人が，ある秘密を打ち明けてきました。彼女がその秘密を朋子（ともこ）に言わないように懇願してきました。このことを She begged で始めて，英語で表現してみよう。

2 コンサートに行ったあなたに，そこのスタッフが列に並ぶように要求してきました。このことを **request** を使って，英語で表現してみよう。

Dictation Section

英語を聞いて書き取ってみよう。その英文の意味も書こう。

1 ____

和訳（　　　　　　　　　　　　　　　　　　　）

2 ____

和訳（　　　　　　　　　　　　　　　　　　　）

3 ____

和訳（　　　　　　　　　　　　　　　　　　　）

Unit 5 Vietnam Chapter 15 Big Dong

Ryu left the wharf for Big Dong in a small boat. There were two rowers with conical-shaped hats on in the boat, but Ryu did not know why two workers were on the boat. He was a little concerned about this form of transportation because the boat was made of woven bamboo and perhaps it might sink into the water soon. He thought the boat was moving toward the destination in the river, but the vehicle was on the 5-meter wide canal, going through the rice fields. Anyhow, Ryu forgot his concerns and was quickly attracted by the beautiful scenery around him. It was one of the magnificent scenes that reminded him of the southern area of China, and the wonderful view impressed him very much. The paddlers seemed to be a mother and her daughter. One of them abruptly asked Ryu about his birthplace in broken English, so he responded by just saying, "From Japan."

He was sure that he was in the middle of the rice fields. As the boat went up the narrow canal, more magnificent views came into sight before

River Close to Big Dong

him. He saw sheer rock surfaces on both sides of the canal. The mountain was made of rock and it looked as if some trees were sticking desperately toward the steep rock. The wonder at trees' ability to survive overwhelmed him. When he looked back at the canal, a few boats were trying to catch up with his boat. He saw female rowers rowing the boats and he wondered what they were trying to do here on the water.

After a while, the canal was divided in the rice fields, so they had to lift their boat into another canal which led to the river. The rowers did not have enough power to do it; therefore, they needed a helper to lift it up. Embracing some complaints about it, helplessly, Ryu helped them with the work even though he was the passenger. They started again for the destination, Big Dong. Ryu saw some children taking photos of his boat from the bank nearby. However, he did not understand at all why they were taking photos there. He was afraid the photos could not be developed quickly there in the rural area, and the pictures would be of no use for the children. And yet, on his way back from Big Dong, the children requested Ryu to buy some photos they had taken from the bank.

Further, on the way to Big Dong, all of a sudden, the rowers quit rowing the boat on the quiet water. It was twenty minutes after they left the wharf, starting point, that they conducted such a mysterious behavior on the serene river. Surely the place where they stopped the boat was in the middle of the lake-like river which was surrounded by steep rock-made mountains with some bushes. Ryu wondered what happened to them and began to glance around restlessly. One rower opened one of the cardboard boxes they had taken on board beforehand and took out some stuff from the inside. However, Ryu did not perceive what they were doing on the boat because he seated himself in the front of the boat, turning back on the female workers.

Then one of them patted Ryu on the shoulder from behind to show the silk or cotton materials to him. Ryu turned back to the rower to see what was happening behind him. At that moment he was amazed to see her arranging the materials on the board close to him. Ryu thought, "What are these? How did they bring the stuff here?" Next moment, gesturing to him, she urged him to purchase the decorated fabrics such as cloth bags and dishcloths. However, Ryu was not at all interested in buying fabrics to decorate around the house. Therefore, even though the Vietnamese rower requested that he should purchase one of them using gestures of putting the material on her hand and bringing it close up to his face, he just glanced at the stuff and at once averted his eyes from it. Even so, she demanded that he should buy different kinds of materials again and again, patting him on the shoulder and using the same gestures. The older woman rower guessed Ryu was not going to buy anything on their boat. Using broken English, she told him that they would not move the boat ahead if he did not buy anything. Ryu was astonished to hear her English and hesitated for a moment, but he looked at her in no time and unwillingly showed her a positive attitude toward purchasing silk goods. At that moment she put it into a paper bag with full smiles on her face. Ryu thought they would be just like swindlers, not rowers.

Again, two women started to row the boat, heading for the destination, Big Dong. Thirty minutes had passed since he had left the wharf by boat. It was so hot in Vietnam that perspiration gradually came out of his whole body. However, he had to endure the sweltering hot weather. He was on the river before he knew it. While the boat was going through a glorious cave, he was impressed to see the grand, majestic views such as stalactites extending down from the ceiling. He was relieved to be in a little cool cave, but the cave was very small. They moved out of this comfortable place in a couple of minutes. The rowers and Ryu took a break on the boat there. That was the beginning of another nightmare.

Several boats appeared from nowhere, and one boat approached his boat and stopped just beside it. Then the women on the boats began to take out some canned soft drinks as if they were reading his mind. Surely it was so hot that he was dying for some water or something. Ryu was trying to buy two cans of drinks for himself. Then one of the women urged him to purchase two more for the two rowers, pointing at them. Although he hesitated to buy them for a minute, he finally bought four canned soft drinks for four dollars. Ryu thought that he was an easy target on the boat because he could not possibly escape from it in the river.

Woman Crossing the Busy Street

Vocabulary Check

英単語に合う意味を右の日本語から選び，(　　　) に記号を記入しなさい。

1 bamboo	(　　　　　)	a. 必死で
2 vehicle	(　　　　　)	b. 荘厳な
3 canal	(　　　　　)	c. 避ける
4 perspiration	(　　　　　)	d. 焼け付くような
5 majestic	(　　　　　)	e. 乗り物
6 desperately	(　　　　　)	f. 仕方なく
7 overwhelm	(　　　　　)	g. 水路
8 helplessly	(　　　　　)	h. 圧倒する
9 avert	(　　　　　)	i. 汗
10 sweltering	(　　　　　)	j. 竹

Listening Section　英文をよく聞いて，英語で答えよう。

1 ______________________________

2 ______________________________

3 ______________________________

4 ______________________________

Reading Comprehension

本文をよく読んで，次の問いに日本語で答えよう。

1　龍が荘厳な景色を見た時，どこの地を思い起こしましたか。

2　龍が船から見た山肌はどのようでしたか。

3　龍は川の土手に何を見ましたか。

4　龍にとって、ここでの悪夢とは何だったのですか。2つ書きなさい。

Speaking Section

本文に合うように空所を埋めよう。但し，下線部には 2 語以上入る。その後，龍（Ryu）になったつもりで，パートナー（A）と対話をしてみよう。

<Part 1>

A: Where did you go, Ryu?

Ryu: I went to ________________________ in Vietnam.

A: What is it?

Ryu: It's sort of a huge (　　　　　　).

A: Oh, really? How did you get there?

Ryu: We took a (　　　　　　) to get there.

A: How was it?

Ryu: It's ridiculous because we were going through a (　　　　　　) in the ________________________ first.

A: Wow! That sounds strange.

Ryu: Let me explain what happened there.

A: Go on, please.

Ryu: You know, on the way, they had to lift the (　　　　　　) up into ________________________. But unfortunately they were not powerful enough to do it, so I had to help them (　　　　　　) it up.

A: What? That's unbelievable!

<Part 2>

A: Was it beautiful around Big Dong?

Ryu: Yes, it was. But I had a (　　　　　　) experience on the boat.

A: Really? Tell me about it.

Ryu: You know, it was very (　　　　　　) there. So we were very (　　　　　　). At that time a few boats (　　　　　　) us and they started (　　　　　　) soft drinks to us.

A: Sounds nice.

Ryu: But they requested that I buy drinks for the (　　　　　　) as well.

A: What? Why?

Ryu: I don't know, but maybe they had to make money.

A: How did you deal with that?

Ryu: I thought it over and over, but I had no idea. Also, I could not get out of there because I was on the ( ). So finally I ____________________ for them, too.

A: Wow! You were an ____________________, weren't you? That was quite an unusual experience, wasn't it!

Grammar Section

受動態の学習をしよう。受動態とは「be 動詞+過去分詞」の形で使用され,「～される（た）」「～されている（いた）」という意味を表す。

The mountain **is made** of rock. （その山は岩でできている。）

Ryu **was** quickly **attracted** by the beautiful scenery around him.
（龍は，周囲の景色にすぐに魅了された。）

He **was relieved** to be in a little cool cave.（彼は，少し涼しい穴にいてホッとしていた。）

The street **was crowded** with Christmas shoppers.
（その通りは，クリスマスの買い物客で混雑していた。）

助動詞がある場合は,「助動詞+be+過去分詞」という形である。can, may, will, must, should, could, might, would など，様々な助動詞の形を見てみよう。

The photos **could** not **be developed** quickly there in the rural area.
（その写真は田舎ではすぐに現像できなかった。）

The building **will be constructed** this April.（その建物は，今年の 4 月には建てられるだろう。）

This medicine **should be taken** three times a day.（この薬は，1 日に 3 回服用されるべきだ。）

Arrange Words

（　　　）内の語を並べ替えて，正しい英文にしよう。

1 When I woke up this morning, (covered, snow, the, with, mountain, was).

2 He (be, of, downturn, fired, the, because, might, economic).

3 The (built, of, the department, building, front, be, brand-new, in, will) store this April.

Writing Section

ここでは次の英語表現を学ぼう。

be dying for～の語句で「～がほしくてたまらない」を表す。他にも，**be longing for～**，**be eager for～**という表現がある。また，**be dying to do**，**be eager to do**，**be longing to do**，**be bursting to do** で「～したくてたまらない，～することを切望する」という意味を表す。

He was **dying for** some water or something.（彼は，水か何かがほしくてたまらない。）

She is **longing to** take a trip to the southern area of China.
（彼女は，中国の南部地域を旅行したくてうずうずしている。）

それでは，学習した英語表現を使って練習しよう。次の状況で英文を書いてみよう。

1　あなたは夏休暇が短いと思っています。もっと長期の夏休暇がほしくてたまりません。このことを dying for を使って，英語で表現してみよう。

2　あなたは中学校時代のアルバムを見ながら，当時の懐かしき，よき時代を思い出しています。その頃の同級生に会いたくてたまらない，ということを longing to を使って，英語で表現してみよう。

Dictation Section

英語を聞いて書き取ってみよう。その英文の意味も書こう。

1 ______________________________

和訳（ ）

2 ______________________________

和訳（ ）

3 ______________________________

和訳（ ）

Unit 6 Canada

Unit 6 Canada Chapter 16 Parade and Town

Dean, who was a coordinator and Robin's husband, showed Ryu around Gibsons in his car. The car smelled of an odd odor, similar to rotten crabs. First off, he drove Ryu to the bar he manages, which was located along the coast of Lower Gibsons. It had a nice sea view of floating white yachts and big green islands dotted with houses, which were a long way from there. It seemed to him that there were usually plenty of customers who visited the bar almost every night. When Ryu visited there, there were no people except the employees, such as a cleaning woman and a cook, because the bar was closed in the morning.

The bar was closely connected to an artificial rock wharf, which was constructed a few years earlier. After Ryu enjoyed the spectacular view, the coordinator drove him to the paper mill factory, Oji Mill, which was close to Langdale Port. He said, "I was born and brought up here in Gibsons, so I have a lot of fond memories everywhere in this town."

When Dean was driving along the coast, he opened his mouth all of a

Sea Cavalcade

sudden, pointing to a certain spot, "This is the place (sea) where we used to swim when I was a kid." Everybody has a lot of memories around their own hometowns. When they walk around their birthplaces, the scenes are reminiscent of their good old days. As for Ryu, there are tons of memories around his house and his hometown in Japan. For instance, looking at the mountain behind his house reminds him of his dear old childhood.

Gibsons holds the big festival called Sea Cavalcade at the end of July every year. Dean said, "We're expecting lots of tourists to visit here so we can earn more money for these three days." Ryu guessed that Dean must be tremendously busy working at the bar during the festival. However, he seemed very happy to make extra money even though he was busy. He was overburdened with his work, but he was totally delighted at the same time.

Dean gave him a black cap with the logotype, *Monson Canadian Light,* on it and a T-shirt with the word, *dame*, in front. Then Robin provided Ryu with two detective stories including a thrilling story which happened in Gibsons, and two cook books which were useful presents for his wife.

His host father, John, very quickly uses the expressions, such as '(She's) off her rocker,' and 'I copped out.' The former phrase was mentioned in the following situation: his wife had lost her temper because he was trying to explain to me about the word 'twit'. At that time he soon voiced "She's off her rocker." The latter phrase was used when he showed his will to refuse to do something she asked for. That is 'I copped out.'

They had the big parade in Gibsons on the 28th. Ryu left home at 10:00 since he was going to see Robin at a camera store in the mall at 10:30. The road was supposed to be blocked off before the parade began. As he expected, local people were prepairing to close off the main road to prevent cars from entering into it. One of the host families had to work on weekends, so Robin promised to take care of the students during the daytime.

It was so chilly then that many local people who came to see the parade wore a summer sweater or a jacket, and they looked warm. One of the Japanese boys wore only a T-shirt, so the boy was always saying, "Cold, cold." Robin offered him a summer sweater. He refused her kind offer at first, which was a typical Japanese way of behaving. Japanese people tend to feel guilty about borrowing clothes from other people who are not their friends. Since it was cloudy and windy, Ryu also felt cold in the morning during the parade even though he wore a jacket.

The parade was held for about an hour. Ryu enjoyed taking photos and looking at different types of floats moving along the road. Interestingly enough, when people on the floats scattered candies around the road, children standing there scrambled to collect them.

Ryu thought that, though this might be stereotypical behavior of Canadians, generally Japanese people have the typical characteristic of being reserved and modest. At a bar or at home when we are asked, "Would you like whisky?" it is hard to refuse it even if we don't want it. However, we think it is good only to drink modestly. Japanese people tend to feel guilty about refusing the other person's kind offering even when they don't want it. People hesitate to respond to kindnesses, especially when they wonder if they may refuse them.

Japanese Girls in Parade

Vocabulary Check

英単語に合う意味を右の日本語から選び，(　　)に記号を記入しなさい。

1 coordinator	(　　　)	a. 波止場
2 dot	(　　　)	b. 探偵の
3 artificial	(　　　)	c. ばらまく
4 wharf	(　　　)	d. 平静，気分
5 spectacular	(　　　)	e. 思い出させる，偲ばせる
6 reminiscent	(　　　)	f. 点在させる
7 scramble	(　　　)	g. 奪い合う
8 detective	(　　　)	h. 調整する人
9 temper	(　　　)	i. 人工の
10 scatter	(　　　)	j. 壮大な，壮観な

Listening Section　英文をよく聞いて，英語で答えよう。

1 ______________________________

2 ______________________________

3 ______________________________

4 ______________________________

Reading Comprehension

本文をよく読んで，次の問いに日本語で答えよう。

1　龍はDeanとRobinから何をもらいましたか。

2　ジョンが「She's off her rocker.」と叫んだのはどうしてですか。

3　龍にとって，パレード中にとても面白いことがありました。それはどんなことですか。

4　典型的な日本人の特徴は何だと言っていますか。また，龍が挙げた具体的な例について述べなさい。

Speaking Section

本文に合うように空所を埋めよう。但し，下線部には 2 語以上入る。その後，龍（Ryu）になったつもりで，パートナー（A）と対話をしてみよう。

<Part 1>

A: Did you go to a bar in Canada, Ryu?

Ryu: Sure. The bar was run by our (   ), Dean.

A: I see. How was the view from there?

Ryu: We enjoyed the spectacular view from there. The bar was closely connected to an (   ) rock (   ).

A: Wow, that's wonderful. Did you go somewhere else?

Ryu: Yes. Dean drove me around the town, (   ). Then we went to a ______________________ factory close to Langdale Port. While driving along the coast, he told me about his ______________________ in his hometown.

A: You had a good time together with him, didn't you?

Ryu: Also, I remembered my (   ) in Japan, especially, my (   ) when I spent time playing in the mountain behind my house.

<Part 2>

A: I heard you joined the festival in Gibsons. When was it held?

Ryu: It was held at the ______________________________ every year. The festival is called _________________________.

A: Ah, huh. Did you have a good time there?

Ryu: Yes. I saw a lot of (   ) and local people marching in the parade holding _________________________ on the street. Take a look at this picture.

A: Excellent! Was it a nice day?

Ryu: Yes, but it was a (   ) day. So we had to wear a __________ ___________________ or a (   ) to keep us warm.

A: Even in ( ) Canadians sometimes need to wear it there.

Ryu: I think the town is ( ) along the coast. That's why it might be a little ( ) and chilly.

A: I see.

Grammar Section

ここでは動名詞の学習をしよう。動名詞は「～ing」の形で名詞の働きをする。本文中の例文で確認しよう。

Looking at the mountain behind his house reminds him of his dear childhood.

（彼の家の裏の山を見ると，子供時代のことを思い出す。）

この英文では，主語の部分で動名詞が使われている。また，前置詞の後や動詞の後にも動名詞が使われる。例文で確認しよう。

They are talking **about traveling** abroad.（彼らは海外旅行について話している。）

My neighbor is **considering buying** an energy-efficient car.

（隣人は燃費のよい車を購入することを考えている。）

また，次のような動詞の後に動名詞を使う。

admit, avoid, consider, deny, discuss, enjoy, escape, finish, imagine, mind, miss, practice, quit, recommend, suggest など。

Arrange Words

（ ）内の語を並べ替えて，正しい英文にしよう。

1 He has a (walk, of, habit, a, good, taking) every morning.

2 You (before, eating, much, too, avoid, should) you go to bed .

3 Although that was my favorite drama, I (this, watching, week, it, missed).

Writing Section

ここでは次の英語表現を学ぼう。

ここでは「**remind～of/about...**」(～に...を思い起こさせる，思い出させる)という英語表現を学ぼう。本文中の例文で確認しよう。

That reminds him of his dear childhood.（そのことが，彼に懐かしい子供時代のことを思い出させる。）

他の用法として，「**remind～that[wh-]節...**」もある。

Please remind me that I owe you ten thousand yen.

（あなたに 1 万円借りていることを忘れていたら注意してください。）

他に，**reminder**（思い出させる人/もの，気づかせる人/もの）を使った表現も覚えておこう。

Just a reminder that you will have no class tomorrow.

（確認しておきますが，明日は授業がありません。）

それでは，学習した英語表現を使って練習しよう。次の状況で英文を書いてみよう。

1　あなたは，カナダへ行ったときの写真を見ています。それを見るといつもカナダのホストファミリーのことを思い出します。このことを The picture... で始めて，英語で表現してみよう。

2　あなたは，クラブの仲間と話をしています。一人の忘れっぽい友人に明後日会合があることになっていることを Just a...で始めて，英語で表現してみよう。

Dictation Section

英語を聞いて書き取ってみよう。その英文の意味も書こう。

1 ______________________________

和訳（　　　　　　　　　　　　　　　　　　　　）

2 ____

和訳(　　　　　　　　　　　　　　　　　　　　　　　　)

3 ____

和訳(　　　　　　　　　　　　　　　　　　　　　　　　)

Langdale Port

Unit 6 Canada Chapter 17 Church

Ryu participated in a Sunday's ceremony at a Protestant church. His host family was quite concerned about their lodger, Chris, who left their house for his new job on an island about one week before. They were originally asked by one of the Christians to let him stay at their home in order to reform him. Chris had a bad habit of drinking heavily almost every night and finally became an alcoholic; what was worse, his parents were also heavy drinkers like him. That was why Ryu's host parents couldn't compel Chris to go home in order to stay away from drinking. People concerned thought that somebody should take charge of him; therefore, the host parents were determined to take care of him until he conquered his bad habit.

On that day the host parents were very irritated because Chris did not show up for some time after they arrived at the church. He was supposed to talk about his story in front of the parishioners. Ryu was sometimes looking around expecting the lodger to come sooner or later.

Preparation for Sunday's Ceremony

However, finally the preacher started to give a lecture on Christianity. The preacher said, "Do what you want others to do," which Ryu supposed was a famous sentence in the Bible. (It reminds him of another famous sentence, 'Love your neighbors.') Come to think of it, it is really difficult to do the action according to the very meaning of the cliché. All of a sudden, while the preacher was lecturing, Chris showed up at the church. Ryu's host parents were very happy to see his figure.

After the preacher's lecture, the chairperson introduced their friend, Chris, to all the participants. Amazingly, he got on the stage to tell his painful and long-suffering story to the audience at the church. While telling the story, he was crying and crying on the stage. Ryu became emotional to hear Chris's sufferings and wept in sympathy with him. Tears were coming out of Ryu's eyes, on and on, in spite of his efforts to stop it from flowing.

"This is a miracle! I was saved by all of you including my host family, John and Anna. I got a job from a millionaire on the island who also gave me a boat and a small house. I have tons of jobs here to make ends meet. Thank you for everything!" Chris honestly said. Ryu was sure this was truly a miraculous thing. John and Anna said unanimously that it was unbelievably a miracle. It was **a bolt out of the blue.**

In the afternoon Ryu's host family showed him around the closest town, Sechelt, where there were some sightseeing places such as an Indian reservation and a beautiful coast. When Ryu walked around the reservation, he saw one of the native people living nearby and approached him to ask him about the reservation and their situations. Ryu knew that they had a sad and terrible history in which they were discriminated against by settlers from Europe, just as Native Americans were. Ryu asked the native person to pose with him for the photograph before they said good-bye.

Next week Ryu and his host family left home for the church at 10: 20 a.m. They had another big ceremony at the church that day, sang several merry songs, and listened to a lecture about Christianity which included the praises of God. The lecturer often said, "God knows everything. God knows you. God knows the past, the present and the future."

After that, they had a holy and magnificent ceremony at the church. The noisy children were forced to leave the hall to keep the ceremony quiet. Unfortunately, Ryu heard some troublesome kids crying out in another room where they were made to stay. The ceremony was officially called Lord's Supper, but they generally called it Communions. In the ceremony people were served a piece of bread which meant a part of Christ's Body and a very small cup of grape juice meaning blood of Christ. By so doing, it was believed that they could be a part of Christ and overcome their sufferings. Ryu had no idea whether it was true or not. People took one tiny piece of bread from the plate with many pieces on it and passed it to the next person. Ryu ate one piece, but he didn't drink a tiny cup of grape juice called Jesus blood. That was because his host mother, Anna gave him a piece of advice that he didn't have to drink it unless he wanted to.

It chanced that Ryu met a black student from Togo in Africa named Dominique, who was staying here in Gibsons to study at university. He got this student's address and e-mail account in order to keep in touch with him.

Singing in the Church

Besides, Ryu happened to talk to an elderly person who had a plastic knee orthosis. The senior citizen asked him where he was staying. Hardly had Ryu responded to him quickly saying, "Mr. Sinke", when the man Joked, "He came here by Titanic." Ryu did not comprehend him and he got mixed up. He noticed Ryu was confused about his words and lost no time to say, "The Titanic sank!" Finally, Ryu understood the pronunciation pun, ‘Sinke and sank’.

Vocabulary Check

英単語に合う意味を右の日本語から選び，(　　)に記号を記入しなさい。

1 enclose	(　　　　)	a. いらいらさせる
2 discriminate	(　　　　)	b. 閉じ込める
3 lodger	(　　　　)	c. 同情
4 originally	(　　　　)	d. 矯正する
5 reform	(　　　　)	e. 元来
6 irritate	(　　　　)	f. 一致して
7 Christianity	(　　　　)	g. キリスト教
8 reservation	(　　　　)	h. 差別する
9 sympathy	(　　　　)	i. 下宿人
10 unanimously	(　　　　)	j. 保護区

Listening Section　英文をよく聞いて，英語で答えよう。

1 ______________________________

2 ______________________________

3 ______________________________

4 ______________________________

Reading Comprehension

本文をよく読んで，次の問いに日本語で答えよう。

1　ホストファミリーは，何故クリスという人物を家に受け入れたのですか。

2　牧師の話を聞いたとき，龍が思い起こした言葉は何でしたか。

3　翌週の儀式のときに，儀式を静粛にするためにどんな手段が取られましたか。

4　Lord's Supper という儀式では，何が行われましたか。

Speaking Section

本文に合うように空所を埋めよう。但し，下線部には 2 語以上入る。その後，龍（Ryu）になったつもりで，パートナー（A）と対話をしてみよう。

<Part 1>

A: Ryu, what is your experience this time?

Ryu: It is about a story at the church.

A: What happened there?

Ryu: I participated in Sunday's ( ) at a ( ) church. Then the ( ), Chris, ( ) my host parents were taking charge of, attended the service there.

A: Did he do something at the church?

Ryu: Yes. He was an ( ) and the host parents were determined to get rid of his bad drinking habit. For that purpose he told the congregation about his ( ) and long-suffering story.

A: What did he look like at that time?

Ryu: He was ( ) while explaining his horrible story.

A: It was a very emotional time, wasn't it?

Ryu: Certainly. I ( ) in sympathy with him.

A: I almost shed ( ) just to hear that.

<Part 2>

A: What happened to Chris after that?

Ryu: He got a job from a ( ) on an island.

A: That's unbelievable.

Ryu: Also, the millionaire provided him with a ( ) and a small ( ).

A: Really? You must be joking.

Ryu: It's true. My host family also said, "It's a miraculous thing."

A: I'm sure Chris is a ( ) guy.

Ryu: I think so, too. I thought at that time it was

a ______________________________.

A: That is a good expression, isn't it? You're a person of wide English ( ).

Ryu: Aw, really!

Grammar Section

ここでは「倒置」の学習をしよう。「倒置」が行われるのは，否定を表す語や方向・場所を表す副詞が文頭に出る場合に起こる。また，仮定法の文の if が省略された場合などにも起こる。本文中の例は, 否定の語が文頭に出た場合である。

Hardly had Ryu responded to him when the man Joked.

（龍がその人に応じたとたん，その人は冗談を言った。）

他にも No sooner～than..., Scarcely～before...などがある。また，if の省略の例文も挙げてみよう。

If he should fail the exam, I will encourage him to try it again.

この英文を倒置の文にすると，文頭が「助動詞＋主語+動詞...」の形になる。

Should he fail the exam, I will encourage him to try it again.

副詞（句）が文頭に出た場合の例を見てみよう。

Only then will we notice that we should do some research.

Arrange Words

（　　　）内の語を並べ替えて，正しい英文にしよう。

1 Hardly (when, someone's, heard, I, had, "help") I headed in that direction.

2 (his, I, number, known, phone, had), I could have called him.

3 No (than, arrived, sooner, station, he, the, had, at) the train started.

Writing Section

ここでは次の英語表現を学ぼう。

ここでは **come to think of it**（よく考えてみれば）という英語表現を学ぼう。ほぼ同じ意味の表現に **on careful thought**, **when you think of it** がある。**on second thought(s)**（考え直してみると）という表現もある。本文中では次のように使われている。

Come to think of it, it is really difficult to do the action according to the very meaning of the cliché.（考えてみると，その言葉の意味通りに行動することは本当に難しい。）

それでは，学習した英語表現を使って練習しよう。次の状況で英文を書いてみよう。

1 歓迎会の企画について話し合っています。あなたは一つの提案をしていたのですが，周囲から次のように言われて反対されました。「よく考えてみれば，それはそもそも（in the first place）あなたの考えだったのよ」と。このことを Come to ...で始めて，英語で表現してみよう。

2 あなたの友人は，先日自動車事故に遭いました。酒の場で楽しそうに振る舞っていたその友人について，「考えてみれば彼も辛かったのよ」という思いを When you ...で始めて，英語で表現してみよう。cf. 辛かった「had a hard time」

Dictation Section

英語を聞いて書き取ってみよう。その英文の意味も書こう。

1 ______________________________

和訳（　　　　　　　　　　　　　　　　　　　　）

2 ______________________________

和訳（　　　　　　　　　　　　　　　　　　　　）

3 ____

和訳（　　　　　　　　　　　　　　　　　　　　　　　　　　　　　　　　　）

Unit 6 Canada Chapter 18 Skookumchuck and Trout Fishing

It was cloudy and black clouds covered almost all of the sky. It threatened to rain at any moment. Ryu was very concerned about the weather, because he and his host parents were supposed to walk to Skookumchuck, which was quite famous for its walking area among the local people as well as the tourists.

It took them about two hours to drive to the entrance of the winding path in Skookumchuck. Before they began to walk on the long path, they went to the toilet. Some tourists passed water in a bush, a little away from the road instead of urinating in the stinky restroom. Honestly speaking, Ryu was among them.

The first several-hundred-meter long road was rather wide and it was nicer to walk along it just after they started to walk. However, they ended up walking in the dense forest where so many trees were covered all over with green moss because of little sunshine. It made Ryu feel as if they had gone back to the ancient times when primitive people used to exist. It so

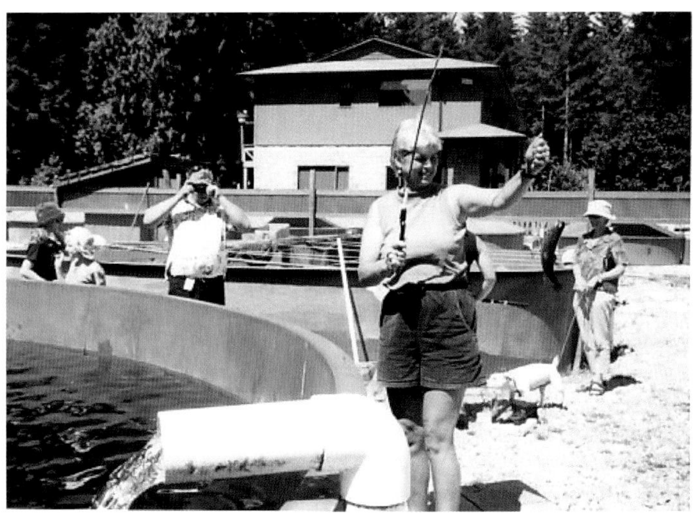

Trout Fishing

happened that they found a big, fallen tree that was thick with moss. It resembled a big poisonous spider, a tarantula.

On their way to a famous spot to see the whirlpool, they stopped by Brown Lake for a while to enjoy the scenery and to take photos of the beautiful lake that was surrounded by luxuriant cedars. Ryu was very impressed to see the trees around the waters' edge reflecting on the surface. They enjoyed walking in the woods and felt refreshed afterwards. In particular, nothing was to be heard except for their voices and footsteps. Even though he stopped and tried to listen for something like animal sounds, he did not hear anything.

They arrived at the whirlpool at around 12:15 after a long walk in the woods. They looked ahead at the sea which looked wavy like a river, spreading out before them.

"Wow! Spectacular!" Ryu shouted. In the middle of the sea was a tiny rocky island as if it were trying to hinder the water flowing down. This caused the whirling to occur there. The size of the whirls was not uniform and they became bigger or smaller. It looked as if the water was alive and it was attacking something. The sight of the flow drove Ryu to another world and made him feel like people were small in comparison to nature. They had a hasty lunch, while looking at the magnificent sea view. Ryu ate sandwiches with ham and butter which his host mother had made for him and instant ramen that Robin gave to him at that time. They were kind enough to prepare hot water to add to the dry ramen noodles.

With regard to Dean's car, it smelled terrible as usual. Ryu dared not to say so himself, as he mentioned earlier, but it smelled like rotten crabs. The first time he got in, he felt uneasy. The more he inhaled the stench, the more nauseated he became. Ryu thought that the same idea goes for other people, including students. Nobody said anything to him. Furthermore, as he expected, the front door of the passenger seat was still broken and tied to the frame with a rope. Therefore, the passenger sitting there had to shut the door roughly.

They went back to Gibsons around 4 o'clock, but they felt fatigued from walking in the woods for so long. Especially, Dean must have felt exhausted from the long walk because of being overweight.

The next day they went fishing for trout at a fish farm. Everybody could fish for trout there. Even a small child was fishing for trout in the water tank. The moment they cast their line in the water, trout bit at the bait. Ryu thought there would be no bait on the fish hook, but he was wrong. Instead of the real bait, a fake lure was put on the hook. He asked an employee about the reason for it. The man said, "We have fed trout here since they were young, so even if the bait is fake and made of rubber, it looks like real bait in its shape and color to them. The shape of the bait is a tiny, black cylinder. You have to pay $2.00 for catching one trout. If you try to catch a second fish, you have to pay another $2.00." Ryu tried not to get accustomed to this easy kind of fishing because people need a lot more patience and skill with real fishing.

After fishing, they got together at Dean's father's house to swim and to enjoy a barbecue party. The house was gorgeous enough to have plenty of big, neat rooms and a bar counter with liquor bottles on the shelves. Ryu wished he could live in such a beautiful and terrific house. Everybody had a lot of fun swimming and talking to each other. After that they cleaned the trout, which was not so easy. The surface of the fish was slippery along with the small intestines.

Tarantula-like Tree Covered with Moss

Vocabulary Check

英単語に合う意味を右の日本語から選び，(　　　) に記号を記入しなさい。

1 threaten	(　　　　　)	a. ひどく臭い
2 winding	(　　　　　)	b. 苔（こけ）
3 stinky	(　　　　　)	c. 原始の
4 dense	(　　　　　)	d. ～のおそれがある
5 moss	(　　　　　)	e. あえて～する
6 primitive	(　　　　　)	f. 疲れさせる
7 dare	(　　　　　)	g. 渦巻き
8 whirl	(　　　　　)	h. 妨げる
9 fatigue	(　　　　　)	i. 曲がりくねった
10 hinder	(　　　　　)	j. 密集した

Listening Section　英文をよく聞いて，英語で答えよう。

1 ______________________________

2 ______________________________

3 ______________________________

4 ______________________________

Reading Comprehension

本文をよく読んで，次の問いに日本語で答えよう。

1　密集した森を歩いているとき，龍にはどんな音が聞こえましたか。

2　龍は Dean の車について 2 つのことを述べています。それらは何ですか。

3　マス釣りで，従業員は本当の餌がなくてもつれる理由は何だと言っていましたか。

4　Dean の父の家はどんな家でしたか。具体的に述べなさい。

Speaking Section

本文に合うように空所を埋めよう。但し，下線部には 2 語以上入る。その後，龍（Ryu）になったつもりで，パートナー（A）と対話をしてみよう。

<Part 1>

A: Did you go jogging in Canada, Ryu?

Ryu: No. We walked around the ( ) forest for one day.

A: How was it?

Ryu: We had a good time taking a ________. But before that walk, I had to go to the toilet. I didn't want to use that restroom.

A: Why?

Ryu: Because it was ( ).

A: Oh, really! But didn't you go to the toilet?

Ryu: Of course, I did. Instead of using the restroom itself, I hid in a nearby ( ), like some other tourists.

A: Oh! That is not what I would expect!

Ryu: Speaking of walking, many trees in the forest were covered all over with ________.

A: Why did it happen?

Ryu: It's because of ________.

A: How did you feel there?

Ryu: I felt like ( ) people appeared there.

A: That sounds strange.

<Part 2>

A: You went to one of the famous spots, Whirlpool, didn't you?

Ryu: Yes. Before we got there, we stopped by a beautiful lake called ________, where we took photos of the beautiful lake that was surrounded ________.

A: That's splendid!

Ryu: Also, we happened to find a big ( ) tree which resembled a

(　　　　　　　　　).

A:　What is it?

Ryu: You know, it is a poisonous spider.

A:　(　　　　　　　)?

Ryu: Yes. Look at this picture.

A:　Wow! It looks just like a big spider.

Ryu: Anyway, finally we got to the whirlpool, where we had a magnificent view. It looks like the water was (　　　　　　　　) and it was (　　　　　　　) something.

A:　Next time you visit there, would you (　　　　　　　　) me in your suitcase?

Grammar Section

ここでは「it」の学習をしよう。「it」には様々な使い方がある。一度出てきた名詞や語句を指して使う代名詞が基本である。また，天候・時間・距離・明暗などや漠然とその状況を指す場合にも使われる。本文中の例文で確認しよう。

It was cloudy and black clouds covered almost all of the sky.
（曇りで黒い雲がほとんど空を覆っていた。）

It took them about two hours to drive to the entrance of the winding path.
（車で曲がりくねった小道に着くのにおよそ 2 時間かかった。）

It made Ryu feel as if we went back to ancient times.
（そのことで，龍はまるで古代に逆戻りしているかのように感じた。）

また，形式主語・形式目的語として使用される場合もある。

I found it difficult to work under him.　（彼の下で働くのは難しかった。）

Arrange Words

（　　　　）内の語を並べ替えて，正しい英文にしよう。

1 It (to, it's, like, rain, going, looks) soon.

2 (will, that, the, is, president, it, reported, make) a visit to Japan.

3 The tofu tastes a little bad. (fridge, though, has, been, the, even, it, in), it must be rotten.

Writing Section

ここでは次の英語表現を学ぼう。

ここでは **get accustomed to～, get used to～**（～に慣れる）という英語表現を学ぼう。本文中の例文で確認しよう。

Ryu tried not to **get accustomed to** this easy kind of fishing.

(龍は，この簡単そうな釣りに慣れないようにした。)

通常，「to」のあとには名詞または動名詞が続く。

I am used to driving on the narrow roads. (私は狭い道路の運転には慣れている。)

それでは，学習した英語表現を使って練習しよう。次の状況で英文を書いてみよう。

1　あなたは大阪の学校へ転校になりました。そこでの新しい学校生活に慣れていることを英語で表現してみよう。

2　あなたは毎朝早く起きて，英語の発音練習をすることに慣れていることを英語で表現してみよう。

Dictation Section

英語を聞いて書き取ってみよう。その英文の意味も書こう。

1 ______________________________

和訳 (　　　　　　　　　　　　　　　　　　　　)

2 ______________________________

和訳 (　　　　　　　　　　　　　　　　　　　　)

3

和訳(　　　　　　　　　　　　　　　　　　　　　　　　　　　　　　　　　　　)

著者略歴

上西　幸治（うえにし　こうじ）

広島大学名誉教授

1957年　広島県賀茂郡高屋町（現東広島市）生まれ。関西学院大学文学部教育学科卒業後，広島の県立高等学校英語科教諭として勤務。その間，広島大学大学院学校教育研究科博士課程前期及び同教育学研究科博士課程後期修了し，博士（教育学）取得。摂南大学外国語学部准教授，広島大学外国語教育研究センター教授，福山大学大学教育センター教授など歴任。

主要著書・論文

『英語教科書の歴史的研究』（辞游社，共著）

「A Study of Factors Contributing to English Speaking Proficiency: Comparing Japanese High School and University Students' Speaking Factors」（『全国英語教育学会紀要』2004 年第 15 巻 pp.119-128）

「A Study of Factors Contributing to English Writing Ability: With a Focus on Two Types of Writing Task」（『全国英語教育学会紀要』2006年第17巻 pp.71-80）

『LONGMAN ロングマン英和辞典』編集・校閲・調査協力（桐原書店）2006年

『Factors in Determining English Speaking Ability: With a Focus on Japanese EFL Learners』（溪水社）2007年

『英語でプレゼン！－基礎から演習－』（丸善京都出版ブックセンター）2009年

『人生、夢に向かってチャレンジ－一歩踏み出せば景色は変わる－』（丸善京都出版ブックセンター）2017年

『めざせ！情熱英語教師－生徒の心に火をつけよう－』（溪水社）2018年

当書籍には、Listening Section と Dictation Section 用の CD、そして文中の練習問題解答編の小冊子がございます。

大学・短大・専門学校等の講義に当書籍をご使用いただいている教員の方でご希望される方全員に無償で差しあげます。ご希望の方は、お送り先のご住所、お電話番号、ご芳名と書籍の簡単なご感想をご記入いただき、ふくろう出版宛郵便もしくはメールでお申し込みください。

Ryu's Misadventures Abroad Revised Edition

2012 年 4 月 2 日　初版発行
2022 年 6 月 2 日　改訂版発行

著　者　上西　幸治

発　行　ふくろう出版
〒700-0035　岡山市北区高柳西町1-23
友野印刷ビル
TEL：086-255-2181
FAX：086-255-6324
http://www.296.jp
e-mail：info@296.jp
振替　01310-8-95147

印刷・製本　友野印刷株式会社

ISBN978-4-86186-854-2 C3082